RAIDERS OF THE CARIBBEAN

TRENT JOHNSTON was a leading cricketer in Sydney first grade when he came to Ireland as a professional in 1995. He later played for New South Wales and moved to Dublin permanently in 2004 when he was first capped for Ireland. He has since played sixty-three times for the country, who he captained at the 2007 World Cup. He is married to Vanessa and has two children, Claudia and Charlie. He works for Architectural Hardware and plays for Railway Union. This is his first book.

GERARD SIGGINS founded and edited *Irish Cricket Magazine* (1984-87) and has written on cricket since 1985 in the *Sunday Tribune*, where he is assistant editor. In 2005 he wrote *Green Days: Cricket in Ireland since 1792* and in 2006 co-authored *Ireland's 100 Cricket Greats* with James Fitzgerald. He covered the World Cup in the West Indies for the newspaper. He is married to Martha Young and has three children, Jack, Lucy and Billy.

RAIDERS OF THE CARIBBEAN

IRELAND'S CRICKET WORLD CUP

Trent Johnston & Gerard Siggins

Preface by Brian Lara

THE O'BRIEN PRESS
DUBLIN

First published 2007 by The O'Brien Press Ltd,
12 Terenure Road East, Dublin 6, Ireland.
Tel: +353 1 4923333; Fax: +353 1 4922777
E-mail: books@obrien.ie
Website: www.obrien.ie

ISBN: 978-1-84717-064-4

British Library Cataloguing-in-Publication Data
Johnston, Trent
Raiders of the Caribbean
1. Cricket - Ireland 2. Cricket - Tournaments - West Indies
I. Title II. Siggins, Gerard, 1962-
796.3'58'09415

1 2 3 4 5
07 08 09 10

Editing, typesetting, layout and design: The O'Brien Press Ltd
Printing: Creative Print and Design, Wales

DEDICATION

To Martha and Vanessa
and our parents and children

ACKNOWLEDGEMENTS

The 2007 ICC Cricket World Cup was an amazing sporting event full of drama, joy and tragedy. The Irish side were at the heart of much of the action, recording two wins and a tie against top professional teams and knocking favourites Pakistan out of the competition.

Raiders of the Caribbean tells the story of that remarkable time, and how Ireland put together a team to take on the world. One sultry night in Guyana we decided it was a tale worth telling and the result is now in your hands. Each of us took turns to tell the story, so the alternate chapters have different voices; the first by the cricket writer, the second by the man who captained the team, and so on.

It was a long road to playing for Ireland in the World Cup, and plenty of people helped us get there.

We would most like to thank all the players who played their part, especially the fifteen men whose commitment and skill made the 2007 Cricket World Cup such a memorable one. They have made this story one worth telling and we thank them for that. There was another Irish team at the World Cup, the one with cameras, pencils and laptops, and we have drawn on them in many ways. Thanks men, you are all in our debt.

We would also like to thank Adrian Birrell, the coach whose vision saw Ireland shock the cricketing world. Thanks Adi, and best of luck in all you do from now on.

There are many people who worked tirelessly outside the ropes, but mention must be given to Matt Dwyer, Iain Knox, Pete Johnston, Roy Torrens and John Wright for their full part in Team Ireland. Our press officer Barry Chambers is a tireless worker for the cause and a talented photographer. He has been a great help in putting the words and pictures of this book together. Thanks too to Paul Mooney, ace bowler and photographer.

We would also like to thank Vanessa Johnston and Anthony Morrissey for their advice and assistance.

A big thank you to a true great of the game, Brian Lara, for the kind words in his preface.

Our employers at the time, Lucan Fabrics and the *Sunday Tribune*, were generous above and beyond the call of duty and we are grateful to Angus Dunlop, Noirin Hegarty, Michael Roche and PJ Cunningham for their support. Thanks also to Paul Barry and Architectural Hardware for continuing understanding and kindness.

Thanks also to all the peoples of the Caribbean who helped make our time there such a memorable one. Their warm welcome helped us through an often difficult period and we have forged friendships that will live on with those we met.

A big thanks too to Michael and Ivan at The O'Brien Press for their enthusiasm for this project and their support when we needed it most. Thanks also to our tireless editor Síne Quinn for her help and advice.

But the biggest thanks of all go to our families, especially those who sacrificed so much. In different ways, Vanessa and Martha are widowed by cricket, and we thank them for everything they have given. Claudia, Charlie, Jack, Lucy and Billy are our children who mean more than anything. Thanks also to our parents who gave us our love of cricket, of sport, and of books. Nothing we can do will ever repay them.

And finally, a big thanks to the incredible supporters of Irish cricket who followed us across the Atlantic and made us feel as if we were at home in almost every game. Their passion was widely recognised by commentators and they were a real highlight of the World Cup. Several supporters contacted us with their stories and we have included some of the more printable ones. Thanks also to Martin Byrne and Mario Rosenstock for permission to quote from their songs inspired by the team.

We hope you enjoy this book and its stirring story of one of the most amazing months in Irish sporting history.

CONTENTS

PREFACE
BY BRIAN LARA

It was a very special World Cup for me, taking place as it did close to home, and it was also my last time to visit the islands to play international cricket. But I enjoyed other things about the tournament, especially how the so-called 'minnows' played – and none more than Ireland.

Ireland have a great fighting spirit in sport. As a people, that's what the Irish are all about – in their soccer or their cricket or in whatever they do.

I have played several times against Ireland and have always been impressed by how hard they fight for every run and every wicket. They taught West Indies a lesson in 2004 and gave us a tough game in Sabina when we met during the World Cup. We showed them great respect after their win over Pakistan and we stayed focused and committed to ensure we beat them.

I was disappointed that Trent Johnston wasn't able to play that day because of his injury. He has been a tough opponent every time we have met, and we had a few drinks in their dressing room after the game.

I met him later that night, outside a Kingston night club, where he and his team were having difficulty getting past the door man. I was delighted to be able to explain who these great players were and ease their passage.

All over the islands I kept meeting people who told me about how great the Irish players and fans were. They really made a huge impression on the peoples of the Caribbean. I think the West Indians and the Irish have a lot in common and the World Cup has helped bring them even closer together.

I wish Trent Johnston and his Ireland team all the best in the future and hope his book is a great success.

1 EXODUS

Vanessa put down the packing case. She had just sealed up the last of the possessions they wanted to bring half way across the world. The rest, accumulated over eight years in Sydney, had been sold or were in a charity shop. 'What are we doing?' asked her husband, looking her in the eye, 'We're leaving our home, selling up, just so I can have the chance to play three cricket matches. Are we crazy?'

Three years later they remembered that conversation as Vanessa packed her suitcase once again in a Jamaican hotel room. The three cricket matches they uprooted their lives for had turned into nine. The cricket team her husband played for had shocked the world by qualifying for the Super Eight stage of Ireland's first world cup. Crazy, maybe, but there are no regrets now for Vanessa and Trent Johnston.

*   *   *

Although it is a game with a low public profile, cricket has been played in Ireland for more than two centuries. The first fixture for which details survive was played in the Phoenix Park in 1792 between the Military of Ireland and the Gentlemen of Ireland, with the future Duke of Wellington one of the participants. The game expanded enormously in the following fifty years and by the 1850s was the largest sport in the country. It continued to be a game played by all classes and creeds in huge numbers until the foundation of the GAA in 1884. The first team representing Ireland took the field in 1855 against its English counterparts and handed them a 107 run thrashing. The sides, however, were not remotely representative of either island, the local players all coming from the upper classes of Dublin.

Various elements combined to send the game into decline. The atmosphere changed in rural Ireland at the time of the Land War (stoked up by Charles Stewart Parnell, himself a leading cricketer with Avondale and Phoenix), and the growth of the Gaelic games benefited from the mistrust between landlord and tenant. The GAA's promotion of a Gaelic nationalist Ireland was not dismissive of cricket – its leading light, Michael Cusack, believed cricket was the best game for children to play, as it taught many useful skills, but the game's association with England was a downside for the Gaels.

The game continued to thrive in many areas however, and all classes in Dublin were able to enjoy the game – notably on the twenty fields available to the public in the Phoenix Park. The second generation of GAA administrators were more closely linked to the new Sinn Féin ('Ourselves Alone') movement and introduced a ban on 'foreign' (meaning English) games for GAA members in 1902. The ban meant that a hurler or Gaelic footballer who was found to have played – or even watched – cricket, soccer, rugby and hockey could be banned from the association. This strict and intolerant ban took more than seventy years to be removed from the GAA rulebook, but the ban ensured that cricket became unknown in much of the country. The game went into even steeper decline in the urban centres of the south with the departure of the British in 1922. Many clubs had regular fixtures against army sides while several also relied on English administrators to boost their memberships. There was also significant Protestant emigration from the Free State in the 1920s that hit cricket harder than most other sports. The game in the north had been strong in the unionist communities and continued to be so, although there were – and continue to be – several clubs in the north-west where religion and political affiliation was far less of an issue.

Although 'Ireland' sides had been playing for more than seventy years, it was only with the formation of the Irish Cricket Union in 1923 that a stable administration was applied to the game. This organisation continued to be Dublin-dominated but the northern unions (The Northern Cricket Union around Belfast and the North-Western Cricket Union around Derry) grew in influence. The first international to be held in the north took place in 1924 and in the north-west in 1934. The Ireland fixture list was short, reflecting a strictly amateur outlook. There were annual games against Scotland and Marylebone Cricket Club (MCC), with occasional visits by English counties and touring Test sides. Every two or three years tours across the Irish Sea were arranged when games against Sir Julian Cahn's XI and the Duke of Norfolk's XI showed the limit of Irish ambition.

The spread of access to BBC television in the 1960s and 1970s brought a whole new audience to the game and the visit of stars such as Geoff Boycott, Ian Botham and Viv Richards boosted attendances at international games. It wasn't until 1980, however, that Ireland played its first competitive game, when it was invited to enter the Gillette Cup in England. It took twenty-four years to win a game in this competition, but by then a new goal had been set with Ireland competing in the qualifying rounds for the World Cup for the first time. The ICC Trophy in Kenya in 1994 showed Ireland what needed to be done, as they finished a disappointing eighth place among the non-test playing countries. Afterwards, the ICU finally appointed a full-time coach, ex-England bowler Mike Hendrick, to the national team, but Hendrick's charges finished an agonising fourth in the Malaysia tournament – and only the top three qualified for the 1999 World Cup in England. Hendrick was replaced by New Zealander Ken Rutherford who oversaw a dismal display in Canada in 2001 when Ireland's ranking fell back down to eighth once again. The ICU took its time replacing Rutherford, but was stung by the coach's parting shot, where he described the Irish club game as 'recreational' and said ambitions of World Cup qualification were 'pie in the sky'.

The union recruited Adrian Birrell, former coach of South African state side Eastern Province. The son of a former first-class player (Harry played for EP, Oxford University and Rhodesia), Birrell himself had a modest playing career. He also knew little about cricket in Ireland. 'I met Niall O'Brien and Andrew White at the Eastern Province Cricket Academy and they told me a little about how it worked,' he recalled. Birrell was a quick learner however, and found much to be encouraged about. He arrived three months before his wife and son, and spent that time criss-crossing the country assessing his task. That summer Ireland were narrowly pipped for the European Championship but by the end of the 2002 season Birrell had identified several of the players he would rely on over the next five years. Four members of the first side he sent out (Andrew White, Kyle McCallan, Paul Mooney and Peter Gillespie) ended up in the Caribbean in 2007, but there were several yawning gaps in his ideal team. Niall O'Brien was plucked from obscurity (he wasn't keeping wicket for his province) into the Ireland team and rewarded his coach with an early century against MCC. 'It wasn't a very difficult decision to select Niall, but it was a brave decision. But I'd seen enough of him to know. He had the attitude. South Africans like fighters. They pride themselves on never giving up. Cricket's not always an easy game and you've got to have guys who dig deep in certain situations.'

Birrell was also fortunate that the Irish economy was in the throes of a boom. The traditional pattern of emigration had been reversed and many of the nationalities who arrived in the 1990s were from cricketing nations. Players from Australia, South Africa, Pakistan and India began to find their way onto club sides, especially in Dublin. Some of these men had first come to Ireland to play cricket as professionals – the Leinster Union permitted clubs to hire an overseas player and most recruited an up and coming rookie.

Trent Johnston had first come across Irish cricket in February 1995. An Irishman called Michael John Solomons had been living in Sydney since graduating from Trinity a decade before, and was asked to undertake a talent-scouting mission for his former team mates in Carlisle, a club that drew most of its membership from the tiny Jewish community in Dublin. Solomons made contact with former England test player Barry Knight, who recommended a couple of likely young guns. On his list was a Campbelltown all-rounder called Trent Johnston. Solomons also spoke to the New South Wales coach Steve Rixon and he, too, mentioned Johnston. 'He gave Trent a great reference,' he remembered. 'I went out to North Sydney Oval to meet TJ, who was playing for New South Wales Colts against Queensland. He was bowling really quick in those days off his long run ... very impressive it was!' Solomons doesn't remember much about the game, or the other players. The NSW opening batsman passed him by too. His name was Jeremy Bray, who lined up alongside Johnston in the World Cup twelve years later.

The twenty-year-old Johnston took five wickets in the match, and Solomons returned the following weekend with the offer of a summer contract. 'I didn't know much about Ireland, although we have some Irish relations called Quilter from around Kilkenny. I had to look up the atlas to see where Dublin and Belfast were before I told my mum: 'I'm off to Ireland for six months,' Johnston recalls. He had spent the summer of 1993 as a professional in the Hornsey club in north London, but didn't enjoy it much. 'I never really liked the way they play cricket over there,' he recalled, 'there were three guys on the team who never spoke to me all season just because I was an Aussie. That was hard for a nineteen-year-old.'

Dublin turned out to be quite the opposite: 'A Carlisle member called Brian Stein picked me up from the airport and we met up with a dozen guys ready to show me a night on the town. I was totally jetlagged, but when you're that age you're up for anything. It was a great night.' Johnston was a shrewd addition to a team with plenty of quality in the batting (Mark Cohen and Jason Molins) and slow bowling (Greg and Stephen Molins) but short of pace. With him as spearhead, Carlisle won the 50 overs league, the young Aussie finishing third in the province's bowling averages with 53 wickets, and eighth in the batting with 706 runs. He returned for another two seasons with Carlisle, but the club folded in 1998 due to the decline in numbers to below 1,000 in the Jewish community. Its Maccabi sportsground in Kimmage is now a fitness centre and the precious cricket square a car park.

The younger Carlisle members preferred to socialise in the Leinster clubhouse, in the heart of bustling Rathmines and closer to the centre-city Saturday night action. When their club folded the players dispersed to various clubs such as Clontarf and Railway Union. But when Johnston returned for the 1999 season it was to Leinster he gravitated – and for more than just cricketing reasons. He had met Vanessa Millard at Leinster in 1995. 'We were friends for about a year before romance entered the equation,' remembered Vanessa, 'but within a fortnight of getting together I had sold the car, rented the apartment, resigned from my job and decided to give Australia a go for a year. I stayed for eight and the rest, as they say, is history.' Vanessa was a cricketer herself – rare in the world of cricket WAGs – having been a first XI player with Dublin University and Leinster, as well playing competitive hockey over the years. The pair returned to Ireland to get married in Ballygarrett, County Wexford in September 1998. MJ Solomons's brother, Harold, was the best man, and the pair returned to Sydney.

As Irish cricket gathered speed under Adi Birrell, his old Carlisle team mate Jason Molins – by now Ireland captain – worked out in 2004 that Johnston was entitled to an Irish passport through marriage. Johnston had been considering a summer contract in Scotland but as soon as the little harp-embossed booklet was in his hands he found himself back in Dublin as player-coach of Clontarf. Johnston went straight into the Ireland team to play Surrey in the C&G Trophy and took a crucial wicket as Ireland stunned the county. It was a result filled with irony as Surrey's coach was Steve Rixon, one of those who set Johnston on the path to an Irish cap a decade earlier. His aggressive bowling and dynamic batting saw him become an instant fixture in the side and took 2-29 two games later as another huge scalp was claimed at Stormont – Brian Lara's West Indians. He joined a side that had some of the New Irish already on board. Fellow Australian, Jeremy Bray, was first capped at the end of 2002 having been in Ireland for six years before that. Andre Botha from Johannesburg, South Africa had been spending the Irish summers in Dublin since 1994 and had first played for Ireland as a permitted professional in the English competitions in 2001. When he naturalised as an Irishman in 2003 he became an automatic selection. A third nation was also represented in the newly cosmopolitan side shortly after Johnston's debut. Naseer Shoukat had arrived from Pakistan with a strong first-class career behind him. He too, settled in Dublin and although he was nearly forty when he was first capped, the Rush postman played an important role in the twelve months he was to spend on the team.

Ireland's results continued to improve under Birrell and Molins. Zimbabwe were beaten by ten wickets in June 2003 with the captain scoring an unbeaten 107, one of the record ten wins that season out of fourteen games played. That summer also saw two more precious debutants: batsman Eoin Morgan, the youngest ever at the time, and bowler Boyd Rankin. The following summer the best one-day side in England, Surrey, were beaten in the C&G Trophy. Six weeks later West Indies scored 292-7 in a 50 over game at Stormont, and were stunned when Ireland cruised past that total with more than three overs to spare. Their total of 295-4 included fifties for Molins, Bray and O'Brien.

These results proved to Irish cricket that the necessary improvements had been made and there were enormous expectations that Ireland would easily clinch qualification for the 2007 World Cup. Since the first World Cup in 1975 the ICC has always reserved at least one place for the non-test playing, or 'Associate' members. East Africa (Kenya, Uganda and Tanzania) and Sri Lanka were invited to the first competition but thereafter the ICC Trophy became the route for Associates. Ireland was chosen to host the ICC Trophy in 2005, which would be its fourth attempt to qualify. With five places in the Caribbean on offer there had never been a better chance.

The early rounds were scheduled for the Belfast area, with the later rounds to be played in Dublin. Ireland was favoured by the draw for groups, avoiding strong nations such as Scotland, Holland, Canada and Namibia. Another major boon for Ireland was the availability of Ed Joyce, the former Merrion and Trinity batsman who had made a career at Lord's with Middlesex. Joyce had not played for his country since the previous ICC Trophy in 2001, when he had finished as the tournament's top batsman. The left-hander had, oddly, never scored a century for Ireland in his previous forty-five internationals, but was in top form for the tournament. He started with 103 against Bermuda, followed with 40 (v Uganda), 115 not out (v UAE) and 60 (v Denmark), on most occasions rescuing Ireland from tricky situations. His brother, Dominick, was man of the match against the Danes at Bangor, when Ireland qualified for the semi-finals and thus clinched a place in the top five – and that coveted place in the World Cup.

Ed Joyce missed the semi-final against Canada, when runs from Molins and the middle order trio of Johnston, Gillespie and White saw them home, but was back for the final against Scotland. In front of a packed, sun-baked Clontarf ground the Scots went off like a train and made a huge 324-8. Bray (70) and Ed Joyce (81) had a partnership of 137 for the third wicket but when they were parted Ireland's reply never reached the required rate. It turned out to be Joyce's last game for Ireland, but not the last time he would take to an international cricket field with these men.

Two other members of that squad never played again, seamer Gordon Cooke, who retired at twenty-nine, and all-rounder Naseer Shoukat. But that summer would also see the controversial departure of another important member of that side, captain Jason Molins. 'I was unhappy with Jason's attitude to training,' explained Birrell. 'I lost patience. During the

ICC Trophy I started thinking about it. Jason's obviously a very good player, but Jason never completed a full tournament for us. He kept getting non-impact injuries, pulling groins and stuff. He wasn't fit enough and he wasn't prepared to get fit.' Birrell's mind was made up however, and he made clear that he 'wanted someone who was prepared to lead in all aspects of the game'. He settled on the man who most epitomised the three-dimensional player he valued: Trent Johnston.

One month after the ICC Trophy final Ireland began another important campaign, the three-day ICC Intercontinental Cup, with an exciting three-run win over Scotland. An abandoned draw against the Dutch saw the team qualify for the last-four play-offs in Namibia that October. On a batting track in the Wanderers ground in Windhoek the batsmen helped themselves, with Eoin Morgan, Jeremy Bray and Niall O'Brien all passing 150. Only three other men previously had made such a score for Ireland in first-class games. The final was one of the greatest recoveries by an Irish side, inspired by the new captain. Kenya racked up 401-4 on the first day, but Johnston declared Ireland's innings closed at 313-4. It was a brave move, but one that looked to have failed at the end of the second day with Kenya 192 ahead with only three wickets down. It was the spin-twins of White and McCallan who bowled Ireland to a winning position on the third morning, claiming the last seven wickets for 48 runs and setting up a famous victory.

The Irish team spent the summer of 2006 gearing up for the challenges ahead. The C&G Trophy, the annual knockout tournament that Ireland had competed in for twenty-five years was now a league of two conferences. All eighteen English counties were divided into North (with Scotland) and South (with Ireland), meaning nine tough games against professional opposition. Birrell set the players a target of three wins, and recruited two Pakistani players, Shahid Afridi and Saqlain Mushtaq, to help achieve it. Both proved a disappointment, although Afridi did contribute 36 runs and three wickets to the only win, against

Gloucestershire at Bristol. The highlight of the summer was the visit of England to Stormont for the first official One Day International since that status had been won in the ICC Trophy. In front of a full-house of 8,500, a Marcus Trescothick century backboned an England total of 301-7, with Ed Joyce making 10 on debut for his newly-adopted country. His brother, Dominick, was bowled by Steve Harmison for 0 in the first over, but Ireland made a good fist of the reply and ended with 263-9 thanks to a fifty by Andre Botha and runs from the tail. The junior Joyce dropped out of the Ireland side shortly afterwards, and was unlucky to miss out on a World Cup place. Batsmen Will Porterfield and Kenny Carroll timed their run well to clinch a spot on the plane, with both making big scores on their first appearance at Lord's. Birrell was all the while lining up the fifteen who would be his men in Jamaica, and although there was some clamour to select Jason Molins, the former captain didn't do enough to change the coach's mind.

Birrell named his squad in September, long before it was necessary to do so. But with an extensive programme of preparation lined up, there was a pressing need for players to secure time off work from their employers. The coach had devised a plan that necessitated full-time commitment from 7 January to 26 March, a period of eleven weeks, and posted it to his players. Back in his office in Glasnevin Trent Johnston flicked through Birrell's document. His eye was taken by the last date on the list, where there was a row of question marks. He smiled and realised what the coach was up to – the obvious thing to write there was 'travel home', but Adi wanted his men to know that there were other options. Playing along, Johnston logged onto the ICC website, and checked out the fixtures for the Super Eights stage. Understandably, he misread the complex draw, but was excited anyway in his belief at who would be Ireland's first opponents in the second phase. He closed his eyes and visualised the toss ceremony before the game. 'Heads, Ricky,' he called, 'We'll bat!'

2 A LAND DOWN UNDER

I was born in Wollongong, New South Wales (NSW), on 29 April 1974, the first son to Trevor and Anne, and younger brother to my four-year-old sister, Tracey. I was supposed to be christened Trent but my Dad got a bit caught up in the celebrations and I was registered as David. As I was always known as Trent, I failed to recognise my name at roll call in my first class on my first day at St Joseph's Secondary School, which was slightly embarrassing.

My father had three brothers and a sister, and the boys all played competitive hockey, rugby league and cricket. My mother too, had three brothers and a sister. One of her brothers, Uncle John, scored a triple hundred in the NSW Country competition as a young man – so there was cricket heritage across both sides of the family. Mum played A grade tennis and netball, she continued playing netball well into her forties with all her pals – 'The Dollies' – as they are known. My sister was a very good hockey player, until I dented her confidence in the back garden by striking her between the eyes with a hockey stick, subsequently knocking her out and giving her several stitches. Growing up in Dapto, a southern suburb of 'the Gong', sport was an important part of my life. I started cricket at a very young age with Dapto Cricket Club, known as 'The Canaries'. I played three seasons on their under sevens and I remember turning up to my first training session where I was just one of at least forty hopeful kids. It was all boys in those days – not like now when women's cricket ranks as one of the fastest growing sports in the world.

In the early years I liked to bowl fast and slog – some might say that hasn't changed. I can still remember being selected for my first game on the Dapto Bs – I got a duck and didn't take a wicket. You have to start somewhere. We always trained and played on full length pitches in those days and I remember thinking to myself 'surely Malcolm Marshall doesn't bowl at 85mph (140kmph) from this distance'. It seemed like an impossible feat. Throughout these early years my skills seemed to develop quickly. At family barbecues we always played cricket, and with plenty of older cousins you either took the bruises or went inside. Thankfully I managed to stay outside.

Another Australian cultural tradition was street cricket, played with two rubbish bins and a taped-up tennis ball. Once again I was always the youngest and to qualify for selection I had to supply the tape in multiple colours. I was always the last to bat – it normally got too dark or I got called in to do my homework before my turn came. But there was always tomorrow and I never gave up. At least I honed my fielding skills during these early years as it was my job to field in front of a busy 'T' junction outside our house. It was on a hill and if you missed the ball you'd have to run for 150m to retrieve it – and be rewarded by a punch from the bowler ...

Throughout my early development I was lucky to be coached by some great local players, who helped to shape me into the player I am today. I can only name a few but among the most memorable were Dickie Dowse, Charlie Fryer, Noel Pratt and David Moore, who coached West Indies on their tour of England in 2007. I remember going to watch my Uncle Jimmy play third grade when I was in my early teens. I played a junior match in the morning, rushed home, grabbed a sandwich and jumped on my bike for Reid Park, the home of Dapto cricket. Jimmy was the captain, and I would always whisper to myself a wish that one of the team had had a late night and hadn't turned up – so that I would get a run out. More often than not, this is what happened and I got to bat at number 11 and field from fine leg-to-fine leg. I didn't care: it was just great to be around these guys and watch them play but, most of all, to hear their stories. I was eventually picked for the thirds – or the 'thirsty thirds' as they liked to be called – as a wicket keeper. Two years later I made my first grade debut for Dapto, batting number eight and still keeping wicket.

My dreams of being the next great Test keeper, like Rodney Marsh or Jeff Dujon, all changed as I started to grow too tall to keep, and bowling became my one true passion. My heroes growing up were the West Indies greats: Malcolm Marshall and Desmond Haynes. Marshall could bowl in-swing, out-swing, off cutters and leg cutters at good pace. If anyone chose Haynes or Marshall as their players on the street or in the backyard, I would pack up my bat and ball and go home. That was something I never budged on. I obviously had my Aussie favourites too, for example, Allan Border and Merv Hughes – but Haynes and Marshall were head and shoulders above the rest in my mind.

Dapto Cricket Club celebrated their 150th year in 2007, and I was named in their all-time First XI. It was a very proud achievement for me and my family: I will never forget where I learned to play the game that has given me so much. Unfortunately, I was in South Africa at the time, preparing for the World Cricket League, and could not be there for the presentation night. Dad picked up my memento but maybe I should have gone back to Dapto for the occasion – things might have turned out differently in Kenya!

As things progressed from under tens to under eighteens I remember thinking that I might have a future playing this game. My parents gave me enormous support, sacrificing so much just to get me from game to game and training session to session. At the time I took it all for granted, and while they loved to watch me play cricket they never pressurised me in any way to take it further. That always was going to be my choice.

In my teens I started making representative teams – at fifteen I was picked in the first Illawarra cricket academy. It wasn't a great time to be there, with older members getting better opportunities to develop and improve their skills. When my scholarship was not renewed I was disappointed but it gave me a real incentive to prove people wrong.

My other true passion, when growing up, was rugby league. Traditionally it was cricket in the summer and footy in the winter and this is how it was for me for eight years or so. I wasn't a bad goal kicking five-eighth (the equivalent of a rugby out-half) or outside centre and I even played a bit at fullback. Many sports stars are discovered through school, but in St Joseph's cricket was yet to be introduced. Rugby league was the main game there and I played for the school for four great years. However, it was fast becoming obvious that a decision would have to be made between the two sports, not least because of the size of the opposition. While I seemed to be growing up they were definitely growing out! So I chose cricket.

My cousin, Matthew Head, was faced with a similar decision ten years later, and he chose rugby league and now plays professionally. He took the bruises too. I talked to him from Jamaica during the World Cup and got a great kick to read Matthew's comments on the Internet. 'Everyone in our family is stoked for him. We're all pretty close so I speak to him a fair bit, and he gave me a call after they beat Pakistan,' he told a Sydney newspaper. 'For a Dapto boy to be captaining Ireland through to the Super Eights series of the World Cup, he's gone enormous.' St Joey's have a cricket programme in place now and even got into the spirit of things by setting up a website for the Cricket World Cup, thanks to Brett Moran, an old rugby mate who is now a teacher. The students sent me messages and that was a huge thrill, not just for me but especially for mum.

After leaving school at sixteen, I went to work for BHP, the steelworks that was the major employer in Wollongong, and completed a boiler-making apprenticeship. This was a means to an end, as I wasn't enjoying school and wanted a few quid in my pocket at the end of the week. I was playing first grade cricket with Dapto still but I knew it was time to mix it with the big boys, which meant playing Sydney grade cricket. I had played two years for NSW Country at the Australian championships and had been named Illawarra player of the year – so I was slowly building my credentials. Before I moved the 80km north to Sydney, I was awarded the Big Brother Scholarship for NSW Country, which entitled me to play for a season in England. The fact that it was an Ashes summer there gave the trip extra appeal. The Australia wicketkeeper, Adam Gilchrist, had been a previous recipient of this scholarship so it was a highly regarded award.

April 1993 was both scary and exciting; it was my first time away from home and my first time on an aeroplane. I was going to play cricket for a club called Hornsey in the Middlesex league and it was also to be my first encounter with Warwick Adlam (Wick), who is now my best mate. Wick was the recipient of the same scholarship from the Sydney area. At the time he was a member of the NSW squad, a quality first grade cricketer and a seasoned traveller. I had heard horror stories of Australian cricketers being refused entry in London and I was genuinely nervous. Wick's idea of settling me down was to steal my passport on approach to immigration in Heathrow. As I emptied the contents of my bag – in front of the immigration officer – I caught sight of Wick on the other side waving the passport with a huge grin on his face. We were to share many great experiences in the future and went on to open the bowling together at North Sydney and Mosman (on the Lower North Shore). North Sydney is 3km from the Sydney Central Business District (CBD) and is directly linked to the city centre via the Sydney Harbour Bridge. It is predominantly a business district and home to a lot of apartment dwellers. As a result the club seems to attract a lot of 'country boys', who have moved to the city either for work or indeed cricket. Mosman is a beautiful suburb which lies about 8km from the city centre and wraps around the harbour. It is most famous for the Taronga Zoo and is home to many sporting celebrities, such as Phil Kearns and Pat Rafter.

I remember well my first taste of English cricket. It was a cold April day and I was wearing so many layers of clothes that I could hardly bowl. It was 'time' cricket so it was as boring as hell. I would bowl between fifteen and twenty overs a day, sometimes more. Overseas players weren't always popular and there were team mates who refused to speak to me the entire season. The years toughen you up but as a young cricketer this was hard for me to understand. It didn't reconcile with the image that I had of life as a professional sportsman.

I played with the late Neil Williams, who played for Middlesex and Essex and who also played in one Test match in 1990. Paul Weekes, a recently retired Middlesex all-rounder, and Tim Abrahams, Sky Sports reporter, were other team mates. I made some great friendships and it was during this period that I also began my, often tempestuous, love affair with Newcastle United. Growing up in Australia we only got one televised football game from England a year and that was the FA Cup final. At the time Spurs were in a number of finals; as Dad was a fan it followed that I took them as my team. In London I was friendly with a Geordie called Richard Thewlis who converted me to Newcastle.

A couple of cricketing days stand out for me at Hornsey. The first was when I scored 152 not out. The opposition had just gone in to bat, when a guy came running across the ground carrying a hessian bag with a 'bobby' in hot pursuit. The bloke had just emptied the contents of a house, which I found out later was four doors down from where I was staying. The second day that stands out was when I opened the bowling with Neil Williams (Nelly). We had batted first and Paul Weekes had notched up an easy hundred. We needed two wickets in the last over and it was to be bowled by either me or Neil. Our captain, Stuart Brown, asked Nelly and he said: 'Give it to the youngster.' I got a wicket with my first ball and another with my last, and we won the game. I ran up to Neil and went to give him a high five when he said, 'give me ten' – and then he hugged me. This memory lives with me and I hope that I have demonstrated the same belief in young players as a senior player and captain. The night ended up with our usual ritual of climbing the walls to swim in the local pool.

I went to Lord's to see the Aussies nearly create history, with three of the top four getting hundreds and Mark Waugh being dismissed for 99. A great celebration followed! Watching two former NSW Country boys, Mark Taylor and Michael 'Slats' Slater, both get hundreds at the home of cricket was a lasting memory. Slats is one of my favourite cricketers – I had the pleasure of playing with him for NSW in 1999. In Hornsey I mainly hung around at the Patels with Cheetan and Sanjay. They were around my age and damn good cricketers. We would talk and watch cricket and eat the amazing curries their mother, Jes, used to cook.

I returned to Australia in September to start the domestic season at Campbelltown. The six months in England had been character building; I had certainly learned a great deal about myself from the experience.

*   *   *

Campbelltown (1994-96) was my first team in the Sydney Grade Competition; as it was only an hour's drive from home it seemed the logical choice. The future Australian players, Shane and Brett Lee, and a host of other cricketers from down my way were there too. Having so many Wollongong boys around helped me to integrate into Sydney Grade Cricket. I started in second grade but after some strong performances was promoted to the top grade, where I made my début in a one-day game against St George, who featured my old mate Jeremy 'JB' Bray. It wasn't the start I had dreamed about – my three overs went for forty-eight runs and I was relieved when Shane Lee told me to take a break ... Jeremy had taken me to the sword, with a couple of no-balls going out of the ground. We won in the end, thanks to a hat-trick by Brett and a hundred by Shane. Somehow I was retained for the next game and never looked back. Grade cricket is a tough game – matches are played on consecutive Saturdays so if you miss out while batting it could be weeks before you get another chance, which makes you prize your wicket. Shane and Brett moved on to Mosman. Shane was an established part of the set-up in the NSW state team and Brett had just made the squad, so they needed to be closer to the city and Mosman offered them the opportunity to do this. Their departure gave me the opportunity to take the new ball, in only my second year of grade cricket. We had a young team with only one player who didn't also play for our under twenty-ones. We didn't win many games but we had some fun mixing it with the best in Sydney. And we won the under twenty-one competition by a mile.

I normally went home to Dapto after games at Campbelltown and this is where the 'Chicken Dance' originated. Those long nights were spent celebrating on the dance floor in the Dapto Leagues Club. One night Jeff Hurd commented that I danced like a chicken and so the now-world famous 'Chicken Dance' was born. I reintroduced it in the World Cup to show those guys that I hadn't forgotten where it all began – I'm very proud of my upbringing in Dapto.

In 1996 I left Campbelltown and joined North Sydney. It was a big time in my life as Vanessa (Vee) had moved to Australia from Ireland to be with me. We had first met in Dublin in the summer of 1995, while I was playing as an overseas professional for the Carlisle club. Vee used to play cricket at Leinster Cricket Club and we had lots of mutual friends. In 1995 however, she was seeing someone else and I was a young twenty-one year old having the time of my life! We were friends, however, and our paths continued to cross through that season and again on my return in 1996. We finally got together during the 1996 Olympic Games in Atlanta. I remember we were in Major Tom's bar – just off Grafton St, Dublin. Susie O'Neill had beaten Michelle Smith in the final of the 200m butterfly – ever since that moment we have been an item and sport has featured strongly in our life.

Within a fortnight we had decided that Vanessa should sell her car, rent out her apartment and come back to Sydney with me for 'a year'. As our relationship was very new we agreed that as we had been friends to begin with we would remain friends if things didn't work out – I promised that either way, I would look after Vanessa in Australia. My mother was concerned about this development on a number of fronts and commented that, 'I hope you'll be in separate rooms when you move in together.' Well it didn't work out that way as we shared a three-bedroom flat in Lane Cove with Graham and Steven Doig. We eventually got our own flat, in the same area, and things progressed strongly for us as a couple. It was difficult for Vee as she knew very few people in Australia, and I was very tied up with cricket. In addition, I was working in a pub at night and often wasn't home until the early hours of the morning. North Sydney was a very 'blokey' club at the time, but Vee used to insist on joining me for a drink after matches and practice. At first the guys used to find this strange but gradually the other girls joined and the culture shifted slowly.

I had four great years at North Sydney that really toughened me up for the rest of my life – on and off the field. There I played with guys such as Graham Sharpe, the Taylor Brothers, Stuart MacGill, Wick and probably one of my greatest sporting influences, Phillip Henry 'Skid' Marks. Skid was one of the toughest guys I have ever played with or against. He would throw me the ball and just let me go, but when things weren't going to plan he would step in and stamp his authority. I put together two consecutive fifty-six wicket seasons on a North Sydney wicket, which would be as hard and flat as a runway until Christmas and then green up after it. It was the place I learnt to play positive cricket, and also learnt to know when to pull back and play conservatively. A lot of my decision-making today is based on Skid's captaincy. We reached two finals and three semi-finals, and were unlucky not to take home silverware. I was selected to play for New South Wales from the club and was very proud of that. My last season with North Sydney was spent in the state squad, so I didn't get much chance to play. But they were four good years of our lives in Sydney and both Vanessa and I made some lifetime friends.

I made my Sheffield Shield debut for NSW in Hobart, capital of Tasmania on 11 March 1999, coincidentally eight years to the day before the World Cup opening ceremony. Jamie Cox always got lots of runs against us and he made 128 that first day. But the worst experience had to be breaking my arm after the second day's play. I had opened the bowling with Brett Lee and with figures of 2-74 was feeling pretty good. The team mini-bus arrived and Brad McNamara – a veteran all-rounder and Steve Waugh's best man – was the designated driver. I was the last to mount the bus but Brad thought I was already on – and drove off. The sliding door caught my arm and … CRACK! I had an X-ray at the time but the fracture wasn't spotted until four days later back in Sydney. I thought we would be another player down when Mark 'Tubby' Taylor came into the physio's room and went bananas. Tubby had been at a function with David Boon so he did not find out what had happened until he returned to the team hotel. He left screaming for Brad's blood. I went out the next day and batted for three overs, making five not out, but watched the rest of the game from the stands. Some début! North Sydney had reached the semi-finals and I had been leading the player of the year awards. As I could take no further part in the season we didn't make the final and I didn't win the award. It was a costly mishap.

After the 1999/2000 season my contract with NSW was not renewed, and it hurt. I knew I hadn't performed as I would have liked but I wasn't alone. The worst part was that I didn't get a phone call from anyone associated with NSW cricket; nothing from the coach, Steve Rixon, or the selectors and to this day I have not received an apology or an explanation for this. I turned up at a fitness session in Centennial Park to be asked: 'What are you doing here?' by my mate, Shawn Bradstreet. 'We have training don't we?' I replied, only to be told, 'But, you aren't in the squad mate, you're not in the final eighteen.' I stayed and took part in the session and on the way home I cried, thinking my world had collapsed. It was left to Vanessa to pick me up and help me to turn it around. But it was hard for both of us because we hadn't seen it coming.

I knew it was a short first-class career in Australia (six games in just over a year, 1999-2000), but as a boy coming from Dapto I would have never expected to play for the best team in the world outside international cricket. I had some great memories – my debut was also the last game played by test legends, Mark Taylor and David Boon. I was on a hat-trick in that first game. I got to play at the Sydney Cricket Ground, the Gabba in Brisbane, and the Adelaide Oval.

It was the second year for state players to be contracted and a draft had been introduced for those squad members that weren't to be retained. Jamie Cox, a legendary opening batsman and at the time the Tasmanian captain, asked me to come to Tasmania. This is the guy who had put me all around the park, but he must have seen something he liked. Vanessa was supportive of the move but our first child, Claudia, had just been born, we both had good jobs, a new house and things were secure. It was an easy decision to say no – but it would have been a gutsy one to say yes. I still think about it now and again and ask myself 'what if?'

Having lost contract income and with a growing family to support, I was forced to re-evaluate my situation at club level, too. The time was right for a new beginning and I found myself playing my final – and most enjoyable – grade seasons, four in total, at Mosman CC. I was reunited with Warwick, who had left North Sydney the previous season. Shane and Brett Lee were still there too, along with Marty Haywood and a host of very good players. Culturally, too, it was poles apart from the acknowledged boys' club that was North Sydney. Families were more welcome and the place had a good vibe. Once again we underachieved as a team, but we had some great fun. In cricketing terms no team achievements really stand out of the four years but the lifelong friendships we made there were and are very special. The amount of texts and encouragement I received from Mosmanites during the World Cup was amazing, and I thank them for that.

I got to captain Mosman in my final year and we won the championship for the first time in the club's history. I scored my first First Grade hundred at Rawson Oval – extra enjoyable as it was against North Sydney. I also got my first hat-trick at the forty-second attempt, with the trio of victims including Michael Slater. The Second Grade team won the premiership too, and I finally managed to win the Bill O'Reilly Medal for the First Grade player of the year. I will probably never get a chance to bowl again with Warwick but Charlie (my son) and Will (Wick's boy) may one day cause some havoc on the grade circuit.

*   *   *

I first came to Ireland in 1995 to play as an overseas professional with Carlisle. My deal provided me with 'digs' and pocket money; so as a twenty-one-year-old lad from Dapto I was delighted with myself. I arrived in Terenure where Howard 'H' Block and Eleanor 'Els' Read were to be my new parents for the next six months. I liked their place so much that I ended up making it my home for two seasons. They had two cats – Hemi (now in cat heaven) and Smutch (the hissing cat). I must admit I wasn't much of a cat fan, but these guys became my little brothers and I remember them fondly.

Carlisle was the first club to introduce overseas professionals into the Dublin scene in 1978 when they brought over the Australian test batsman, Julian Weiner. The club was the centre of the local Jewish community and traditionally tennis, bridge, football and rugby were played at the Carlisle ground at Kimmage. There were fifteen senior clubs in Leinster – all in Dublin – and a competitive league and cup structure. Carlisle won a trophy in my first season, by beating Malahide on their ground with the veteran Stephen Molins – uncle of Greg and Jason – and me both getting 70s in a total of 250. 'Big Syd' managed figures of 3-38 and was given the Man of the Match award. What a day! I also remember the last game of the season against YMCA in

Sandymount. YMCA had to beat Carlisle to have a chance of winning the league ahead of Clontarf, but unfortunately for them it was one of the best games I ever bowled in Leinster cricket. I took six wickets that day for Carlisle to deny YMCA the crown and give the title to Clontarf.

A trend started that year that, every Thursday, all the professionals would gather at Major Tom's bar for a night out. It soon picked up pace and became the highlight of the week, with guys coming together from both sides of the Liffey to talk about home and listen to some good old tunes. Harold Solomons, who was later my best man, had taken the summer off from his day job, so he took me around Dublin and showed me the sights. We had a superb week-long break in the Greek islands where we were joined by Gareth 'Gomma' O'Meara of Railway Union. He had such a good time that Gomma thought he had been in Crete when we had actually been in Corfu.

My contract was renewed by Carlisle, and I returned in April 1996 for another season, but once again we ran into a rampant Clontarf side and ended the season without a trophy. The highlight on the field was winning an Irish Senior Cup tie away to Bangor. We were missing five regular team members, and as a consequence the average age of the team was in the late thirties or early forties. With one wicket left, the two runs required for victory came from a French cut off Dr John Simon's bat. If the term 'French cut' sounds impressive, I'd better explain that it refers to a streaky inside edge that just misses the stumps. That was a wonderful moment. I took home more than memories that year as Vanessa and I had decided to set up home in Australia.

In July 1997 I proposed and Vanessa accepted! We had been a couple for only a year but our relationship had been express from the start and we had already shared a lot. We knew from a practical perspective that the following Irish summer my parents, my sister and her husband would be in Europe, it seemed like a good chance to have them at our wedding. We would also use the opportunity for me to play another season in Carlisle as an overseas pro. 1998 was to be the end of an era for

Carlisle Cricket Club, as the members had decided to sell the grounds as dwindling numbers were making its existence harder to justify. It was a sad time for everyone who had been involved with the club over the years but we gave the place a good send-off. It was nice to have my family there that day, as they were travelling around Ireland in the lead up to our wedding. In the end my parents, sister, brother-in-law, uncle, aunty, cousin and cousin-in-law all made it to Ballygarrett, County Wexford on 19 September 1998. Vanessa's parents (Rob and Pat) live in this small village and we love spending time down there. It was a great day but a very emotional occasion for us as we were moving permanently to Australia the following Tuesday, as I was expected at North Sydney the following Saturday, for the first game of the Grade season.

One highlight of the 1998 season was a game in Clontarf when I played for the Leinster Professionals against the Ireland team who were heading to Toronto for the ICC Trophy. The Leinster Professionals XI included myself, Jeremy Bray, Andre Botha and Naseer Shoukat. Andre made a hundred for the Pros (he was dropped six times) and we ran out pretty convincing winners. It was ironic that seven years later we would all be playing for Ireland against a Professional team from the Belfast area in preparation for the 2005 ICC Trophy.

Three years went by and we did return to Dublin in 2001. I had experienced the highs and lows with NSW and needed some time away from the scene to clear my head. Vanessa was delighted to take up the opportunity to spend some time with her family, as Claudia was then just under a year old. As Carlisle was gone, I moved down the road to play with Leinster Cricket Club in Observatory Lane, Rathmines. This is where Vee had played cricket and where we had always socialised in my Carlisle days, so it was the obvious place to play. It was a good season for me personally but not great for Leinster as we failed to gain promotion. It was still a really enjoyable time playing with Jonesy, Gav, JP and Brownie, a really good bunch of guys.

It was funny how the next stage in our life unfolded. We were always told that for me to qualify for an Irish passport I would need to complete the four years residency requirement. However, we discovered that there was – at the time – a well-kept-secret clause called 'post-nuptial dependency' that would enable me to apply for citizenship based on Vanessa's heritage. We knew that if we could pull this off we could move back to Ireland and chase the dream of playing in a World Cup. So we followed up, filled in the forms, enlisted the help of TDs (a special thanks to Paul Keogh, Fine Gael TD for Wexford) and chased the application until we were successful. There was still the small matter of finding a club; jobs and a place for our growing family to live. Charlie had been born in June 2003, so we now had two young children to consider. Clontarf were very helpful in relocating us and at very short notice. I knew that I was a lucky man as, on a warm day, Castle Avenue is the nicest place to play cricket in Ireland.

Now all that was left was to say goodbye to friends and family. It was a very emotional time for my parents – it was hard for them to understand what I was doing, as at this stage qualifying for the World Cup was still to be achieved. We were moving so far away (and taking their grandchildren away from them) for something that was so intangible. I know now that they understand why we did what we did. Hugging my dad in Sabina Park, after the Pakistan victory, I was sure then that he understood. I know, too, that both my parents couldn't be prouder of all that I have achieved with Irish cricket. It took them three days to travel to Jamaica from Australia and they wore the shamrock with as much pride as those supporters born and bred in Ireland.

My first game for Ireland, in April 2004, was a landmark victory over a star-studded Surrey team, coached by Steve Rixon. As he was the guy who didn't renew my NSW contract I obviously took extra pleasure from that victory. We then headed off to Utrecht to play a three-day Intercontinental Cup game against a cocky Dutch side. We quickly cleaned them up with Andy White getting 150 while I got sixty and five wickets. That result meant that we only needed a draw in Clontarf against Scotland later on in the season to qualify for the semi-finals. Sadly we lost on a green seaming wicket when a flat one was what we were looking for. We ended up finishing second at the European Championships, but by beating Scotland, Holland and Denmark we were crucially ranked number one for the ICC Trophy the following year, which ensured an easier draw. We also beat the mighty West Indies in Belfast and nearly overturned Bangladesh in Limavady.

My first season with Clontarf saw us make the semi-final of every competition but only bring one trophy home, when we had a convincing win in the sixty over Antalis Cup against Rush. The biggest disappointment was not being able to play in the Irish Senior Cup semi-final. I was diagnosed with stress fractures in my back and I had to watch from the sideline as my pal Peter Gillespie got Strabane over the line. The year of 2005 dawned and marked into the calendar under June was what all this was about. The ICC Trophy was the qualifying tournament for the World Cup and as it turned out we knew we had qualified once we beat Denmark at Bangor. At that stage the only thing that remained to be decided was in which Caribbean group Ireland would play. After we beat Canada in the semi-final we knew that whoever won the final would play in St Lucia in a group that included Australia and South Africa, while the loser would earn a trip to the home of Bob Marley to play the hosts plus Pakistan and Zimbabwe. Scotland got the better of us that day by forty-seven runs and deserved their title. But our prize was the chance to play in a weaker group with a real chance of picking up a win or two. My own prize was a dislocated shoulder attempting a catch, but our dream had been achieved and we were on our way to the World Cup.

In late October 2005 I was given the captaincy and I was overjoyed with the prospect of leading the team. As captain I would work closely with our coach, Adrian 'Adi' Birrell, to identify and develop the team that we would take to the Caribbean in 2007. My first job as captain was to lead the team to the ICC Intercontinental Cup in Namibia, where we joined Kenya, Bermuda and the United Arab Emirates (UAE). I won my first toss as captain against UAE and elected to bat on a flat wicket in Windhoek. A team could bat ninety overs in their first innings, and we got off to a great start with Dom Joyce and Jeremy 'JB' Bray putting together a hundred partnership. The highlight for me, though, was the way Eoin Morgan constructed his innings of 151 off 150 balls. His control and shot selection belied his years and his performance in this tournament confirmed to me his potential. I picked up five wickets in the first innings coming off a shorter run, with good support from Paul Mooney and Kyle McCallan. Then came my first big decision: do I enforce the follow-on or bat and bat and bat? With our place assured in the final I decided on the latter, allowing the bowlers to put their feet up and the batsmen to have some fun. They certainly did that with JB getting 190 and Niall O'Brien 176. This was more than a rookie captain could have asked for. We fell two wickets short of outright victory – but our first innings led us into the final.

It was 27 October and our opponents, Kenya, made 401-4 with Steve Tikolo getting 177 not out. Unfortunately, I suffered a dislocation and fracture of my right ring finger. I got an injection to try to stay on the field, but couldn't bowl with any control and was a liability. Kyle stood up to the mark again and led the guys well on the park, but we knew we were behind par and that I was unlikely to be able to bat. Whilst walking around the ground, cricket journalist David Townsend asked me, 'Why not declare now, bowl them out and back yourselves to chase them down?' With the way the points system was set up, I knew we would only die a slow death if we didn't do something. Adi and I spoke with the team and we agreed to declare at the next fall of wicket. Niall made his second hundred of the week and I declared our innings closed – for the first time Kenya were on the back foot. They hadn't been expecting this at all. Two of their top order batsmen were off the field and were thus not allowed to bat in their normal position, and for once they looked flustered. At the close of the second day's play Kenya had requested they come off for bad light. If anything, we should have come off for bad sunlight, as the conditions were certainly good enough to finish the overs. Steve Tikolo, their leading batsman and arguably the best batsman outside of test cricket, was at the crease and looking dangerous but they clearly felt that they needed the time to regroup after a dramatic day. There was significant tension as the match was so evenly poised.

The third and last day of the final started well, we took regular wickets and dismissed them for 156, with Kyle doing a great job to get rid of Tikolo and return figures of 4-43. We needed just 244 for victory. All the batsmen got runs, but it was Jeremy with 64 and Andre with 43 not out that stood out. It had been a long time coming – but Ireland had won their first international trophy and it felt really good to have been captain on this trip as I learnt a lot about myself – and cricket. We partied hard into the night, with the trophy never far away. And always full of something resembling alcohol. The supporters that had made the trip were celebrating as well. It is pretty well known that the Irish are great followers of sport, but the people that support Irish cricket are truly amazing. A special mention must go to the 'North County 4'. This was the perfect way to finish the season and the perfect opportunity for us to spend the fines we had raised throughout the season.

We had another extensive programme laid out for us in 2006, with nine Cheltenham and Gloucester (C&G) games against the counties, the start of our defence of the Intercontinental Cup, our first One Day International (ODI) against England, and the European Championships. We failed to deliver in the C&G games but had a good win over Namibia in the Intercontinental Cup at Clontarf. The highlight of the season was against England at Stormont, Ireland's first ODI – and the biggest game in our cricket history up to that point. A crowd of 8,500 turned up and the weather was great. I went head-to-head with an old Mosman team mate, Andrew Strauss, who was England's captain that day. It was also Ed Joyce's first game for England, so the stage was set for something special. Thanks to a Marcus Trescothick hundred they posted a very good 301 that we did our best to chase down. Andre made 56 and a late order flurry got us to a respectable 263 for 9. It was quite an experience facing those guys, and it gave us all an insight into what we might expect in the Caribbean.

At the European Championships in Scotland we beat Denmark, Scotland and Italy to set up a showdown with the Dutch. We posted 274 with Andre, Niall and Kyle all passing 50. We had them on the rack at 49-5 before their star player, Ryan ten Doeschate, came out all guns blazing. Happily the rain finished the game with the Dutch 125-5 off 19 overs and a 'no result' gave us the title. It was a European Championship 2006 clean sweep for Ireland as we won that title at every age group (under thirteens, under fifteens, under seventeens, under nineteens, under twenty-threes and seniors) for the first time in history.

We finished the successful season by playing Scotland in Aberdeen in our penultimate fixture in the Intercontinental Cup. We were pumped up about defending our title and ready for our old adversaries. The game was a farce and extremely frustrating for all of us. Rain and inflexible groundsmanship caused the game to finish two days early. David Langford-Smith had taken five wickets in the first innings and we had Scotland 24-4 in the second, a great position to be in, but the match was controversially abandoned. In order to stay in the competition we had to hope Scotland would fail to beat the UAE, and we would then have to beat the UAE in Abu Dhabi. That didn't seem possible – but only time would tell.

3 THE MAN WITH THE PLAN

Adrian Birrell was a man with a plan. He had impressed his players with his vision, commitment and hard work, and by the time he got to eat his last Christmas dinner as Irish coach he knew they would do anything for him. There were just a handful of days left in chilly Dublin before he would head south to Port Elizabeth, the South African city that had been his home for almost twenty years. Although he would be staying in the house he had kept there, close to his family, this was not a seasonal social visit. He was bringing nineteen Irishmen with him, and they had work to do.

Birrell was born in Grahamstown, 145km east of Port Elizabeth, in 1961 and had what he described as 'a very sheltered upbringing'. His parents were teachers and he went to private school. He had an inkling that all was not well with the apartheid regime in South Africa when he was called up for compulsory national service at the age of eighteen. He told Ian Callender of the *Sunday Times* about an incident that had a profound effect on him and his life. 'We were on the Namibia/Angola border lying in ambush. Thirty-six of us waiting for one guy to come across the road. The platoon was ready to fire. Thankfully it was the first time the "enemy" didn't cross the road.'

Towards the end of his two-year stint he was made an officer and began reading about how the world saw his native land. He moved to Port Elizabeth on a sports scholarship where he met an Eastern Province cricket official called Flip Potgieter who asked Birrell, a fluent Xhosa speaker, to go into the poor black areas and spread the game. 'Politically, Potgieter was ahead of his time. He became an ANC member before it became fashionable and he was labelled a sell-out at the time. But he got hold of me and got me coaching in the townships.' Long before apartheid was abolished, Birrell's township club the Cadbury Cavaliers were playing – and beating – the established white clubs. He was at the heart of a historic moment in South African sport when two of the boys he developed became the first black players to represent the country at schools level. 'That period in my life gave me a fantastic grounding for what has followed, and taught me so much. It was a thoroughly enjoyable experience, and one of which I have terrific memories', he recalled.

The former Eastern Province all-rounder's low-key playing career ended in 1997 (he played 45 first-class games with various EP sides, averaging 21 with the bat and 30 with his leg-breaks) he became a full-time coach, first with the development programme and then as coach of his former province. With EP Cricket he helped develop a coaching structure and when he took the top job at St George's Park he oversaw definite improvement in their one-day results, twice reaching the national final. Ireland was his first job outside South Africa, and he was able to continue to apply the principles he had learned. A superb man manager, Birrell is a naturally humble individual, and passionate about having his players take responsibility and join in decision making. On his arrival he outlined his aims: 'It's getting everyone working in one direction, making sure everyone is goal orientated to get Ireland towards the World Cup, is happy and motivated towards working towards the big picture.'

Birrell brought a modern approach to coaching that invigorated his players. He went to India to seek out a match analysis software program called Scoremate and went to the ICC for more computer aids. These helped him assess areas such as performance, physiology and movement which improved the players and their decision making. Simpler techniques also impressed the squad. 'One day we turned up at nets and Adi had a bucket of water into which he dropped the balls', recalled Jason Molins. 'We didn't know what was going on until he explained that the chances were that we would have to play some games in wet conditions and it made sense to practice with the ball in a damp state.' The squad all had their eyesight measured and continuously monitored over the years, with special prescriptions given to all players for their match sunglasses.

Birrell spent most of the autumn of 2006 in one-to-one sessions with his players. The chosen fifteen worked on their own fitness – Johnston and Langford-Smith met three times a week for punishing games of squash – in core-strengthening programmes devised by physio Iain Knox. Birrell and his backroom team worked with the squad as a whole one day a week, usually in North County, but once a month the sessions were held in Queen's University Belfast to facilitate the northern players. In one important way those players were more fortunate than their compatriots from south of the border. The Sports Council of Northern Ireland paid their salaries for four months, allowing White, McCallan, Rankin, Gillespie and Porterfield to train full-time at the Institute of Sport in Northern Ireland (ISNI) under Australian Rules coach Andy Lavery. Four of the squad were missing for six weeks, guests of the ICC at a winter training camp in Pretoria run under the High Performance Programme. Birrell told the quartet – Kenny Carroll, Kevin O'Brien, John Mooney, and William Porterfield – 'It's a wonderful opportunity for you all to improve both your techniques and fitness levels. One only has to look at the improvements in players who have attended this and similar camps in the past. This time last year Kenny Carroll was very much on the fringes of the Ireland set up, and now he is a vital part of our squad. I hope you use the camp wisely, and get prepared properly for a vital three months in the history of Irish cricket.'

*   *   *

The last day of training in North County was Friday, 5 January 2007, when the team met up with Jeremy Bray after a three month break. 'JB' had spent the winter down under, playing First Grade for Sydney side UTS-Balmain, for whom he scored 313 runs in 11 games, with a best of 90. He had a testing reintroduction to Ireland, undergoing a gruelling one-to-one session with Birrell to assess his form and fitness.

Just after 11.00am on Sunday morning the squad flew out in two groups from Dublin and Belfast. The seven-man northern contingent was done no favours by former sponsors British Midland, being hammered for £640 (€940) excess baggage charge for the short hop to London. At 6.00pm they took a South African Airways flight to Johannesburg, arriving at 7.00am on Monday, connecting with the two-hour flight to Port Elizabeth on the south coast. They would get used to airline food over the next three months – their total air miles were close to 30,000 miles, more than the circumference of the earth.

The first week was a mixture of team-building and work, based near Grahamstown at the Amakhala Game Reserve, which is owned by Birrell's family. The players were royally entertained by Adi's Uncle Bill, who runs the facility on the site of his former farm. 'Bill had an incredible story for every day of the week', explains Trent Johnston. 'He told us about the old days when men would travel two or three hours on horseback to play cricket. One guy would always get blind drunk and get the horse to bring him home. He would sleep on the horse's back and wake up whenever a gate needed to be opened on the way.' The players were frequently entertained in the early stages of the trip, which usually meant a traditional South African *braai*, or barbecue. To their dismay they discovered these usually started at 10.00pm or 10.30pm, which meant that after a hard day's training they were starving when it came to eat. With training beginning again at 8.30am they also had to be careful not to indulge too heavily in alcohol. 'We had one day training at the local cricket ground where it was boiling, 38 degrees they said, so that was all good for acclimatisation and the fitness,' said Kyle McCallan. 'Otherwise we were at the game reserve, practising our throwing and catching on the lawn outside the guest houses. Generally just getting into the swing of things.'

The training went up a gear in the second week with lengthy and intensive net practice at the University of Port Elizabeth. Former England bowler, and sometime Ireland coach, Mike Hendrick arrived on Tuesday, 16 January with Birrell's assistant Matt Dwyer and Leinster development officer Briain O'Rourke. Hendrick worked with the eight quicker bowlers, putting them through their paces at extended net sessions of sixteen overs each. 'Mike is an "old school" coach', explained Johnston. 'His philosophy is that you've got to keep bowling to get your fitness up. He used to say to us "Get you legs right". Hendrick also spent time discussing his theories of the craft, giving bowlers and the captain options for most eventualities that could arise. Adi Birrell was delighted with the generosity of the local union: 'we were given outstanding facilities and we trained really, really hard. We put in the hard yards then and we reaped the rewards from that. Eastern Province Cricket were outstanding in what they provided.'

The party spent eight days in three adjacent houses on the outskirts of Port Elizabeth – the family homes of Birrell, his mother, and sister. The players were amused by the photographs on the walls of their coach in his early twenties sporting luxuriant facial hair. So taken were they with the look that the next few weeks were spent competing to see who could grow the best beard/moustache combo. With spectacularly bad timing, the ICC's photographer arrived to take the official photographs before the contest ended – which is why the TV profiles, match programmes and magazines all showed Johnston and John Mooney with Zapata moustaches and Carroll, Gillespie, Porterfield and Langford-Smith with faintly ludicrous beards. All through the World Cup the players would look up at the stadium big screens to see their private joke paraded before the world.

The final week in South Africa was spent playing four practice matches against various Nelson Mandela University and Port Elizabeth XIs in the UPE grounds and, under lights, at St George's Park. The first game was lost but an opening stand of 183 between Jeremy Bray (89) and Kenny Carroll (100) levelled the series. Birrell was happy with the headache caused by the Railway Union rookie: 'Kenny continues to impress, and I'm delighted for him,' he said. 'It's the result of hard work put in over the last few years, and his time at the ICC training camp has taken his game to a completely new level. It gives me plenty of options both at the top and in the middle of the order.' Bray made another 89 in the third game, which also saw fifties for John Mooney and Niall O'Brien in a 304 a-side tie. Kyle McCallan and Kevin O'Brien bowled Ireland to victory in the final game and a 2-1 win in the mini-series. With most players getting wickets or some batting time in the middle, the main concern as the squad readied themselves to leave Port Elizabeth was the fitness of the skipper. Johnston had fractured a finger early in the 2006 season and after taking eight wickets in the first two games took a blow to the same finger and went to hospital for an X-ray. That revealed severe bruising but no break and he was rested for the final game. The top digit of his right ring finger veers off at a forty degree angle and Johnston expects he will have it lopped off when his cricket career is over. 'There's arthritis in the joint and I've been told the best solution is to chop it off. I'm going to stick it in a jar beside the ball I took five-for to win the Intercontinental Cup with!' It was commitment like this that first attracted Birrell to Johnston: 'What I look for most in a player is attitude', explained the coach. 'Obviously talent is important but I need to know that if we get into a scrap they're there for you. Trent brought that. He's a fighter on the field. He leads on the field and he leads off the field. He leads in training. The guys needed to be pushed. You don't get any glory without hard work. And we needed the hard work.'

On Saturday, 27 February, the team flew north to Nairobi, where they were based at the Hilton Hotel. The Kenyan capital is one degree south of the equator, with an average February temperature of thirty-seven degrees. Playing five One Day Internationals in seven days against their fellow associate members is a hectic schedule in any climate. In the hottest month of the year in equatorial Africa it bordered on brutal. Ireland had played there once before, in 1994, their first appearance in the World Cup qualifying tournament. In those early days of sport science the side's fitness was found wanting and they wilted to an early exit.

The players stayed at the Hilton, and were amused by the so-called 'high security'. The underside of their bus was scanned, and individuals asked to walk through an airport-style scanner. But their enormous mound of luggage was carried around the side, bypassing the machine. The opening World Cricket League (WCL) fixture saw Kenya hammer Scotland, a result that ensured Ireland rose to the top of the Associate one-day rankings for the first time. These were early days in the International Cricket Council (ICC) ranking system, an attempt to put structure on the Associate members, but it was heartening to have reached the number one spot and it confirmed the view of most observers that Ireland were favourites for the World League. Training went well, and Birrell, Dwyer and Johnston sat down on the outfield to discuss selection for the first game against Scotland. 'Most of our debates centred on John Boy and Andy White', revealed the captain. 'If I was picking any team I'd have John Boy Mooney beside me. For his guts, courage, ability, determination and fitness. He needs to be a bowling batsman though, and at the moment he's a batting fielder who also bowls. That day we went with John but once Boyd came in, in Jamaica, John Boy kept losing the selection debates to Andrew.'

Bray scored 116 against Scotland, and Johnston blitzed 45 off 19 balls as a total of 280-7 was posted. It was a massive score but the Scots passed it off the last ball of the game. The decisive moment was a huge hit by Neil McCallum which was caught by Will Porterfield at deep fine leg. With the batsman halfway back to the pavilion umpires Tony Dill and Darrell Hair conferred, and decided the fielder had brushed the rope. McCallum was recalled and his score moved up to 99; he duly passed the century. The bowlers were again off-form against Bermuda, with the innings held up for four minutes during the call to prayer at the neighbouring mosque, but another gutsy century by Porterfield ensued the game was won with eight balls to spare.

There can have been few more prolific days in Irish cricket history than Friday, 5 February, but one that ultimately saw heartbreak. The euphoria began at 6.28am when early risers back home saw Ed Joyce deliver his first century for England and collect the man of the match award in his adopted country's first win of their dismal tour of Australia. Later that morning, William Porterfield (102*) and Kevin O'Brien (142) also made centuries in hoisting a huge target against Kenya. O'Brien hit six sixes and 11 fours in an innings that lasted 125 balls. The total of 284-4 should have been more than enough but the Kenyans took advantage of some wayward bowling to stay close to the required rate. However, with McCallan and Botha taking four wickets each the Kenyans needed 54 to win with the last pair at the wicket. Sadly Thomas Odoyo and Hiren Varaiya nurdled and scampered their way to within sight of the total. With two overs left they needed 19 to win when Johnston asked Langford-Smith to bowl. A single to Varaiya was followed by Odoyo clubbing 6, 6, 4, 4 off successive balls. Langford-Smith left the ground in tears and did not emerge for the presentation. Birrell was also upset: 'Our bowling at the death has been a problem and it has now cost us two vital matches.' Johnston was concerned about his friend, too. 'It was lucky I was rooming with DLS as he was very down. He was really hurting. We now couldn't win the competition and wouldn't qualify for the first 20/20 World Cup. The only thing I could do was summon the players to my room and get the drinks in. Collectively we regrouped. We had no choice.'

'It's very difficult,' said team manager Roy Torrens. 'We prepared so well for this tournament. We trained so hard. These teams here are so evenly matched that when it comes down to the last over, it's the rub of the green and I think, in fairness, we haven't had the rub of the green in the two close matches.'

Another enormous score – 308-7 – was hoisted against Canada, thanks mainly to a century by Eoin Morgan, and again it was overtaken by the opposition in the final over. And a fourth close game was lost, with the Netherlands making 260-7 and Ireland falling six runs short. Johnston was absent with a bout of the stomach illness that hit most of the teams in the competition. Johnston was luckier than Scotland left-arm spinner Glenn Rogers, who was flown home suffering from typhoid. Porterfield (84) and Morgan (94) put on 153 for the second wicket but Ireland never recovered from a dismal collapse from 195-1 to 202-5. Birrell was shattered by the succession of defeats, which meant Ireland finished fifth of six in the final table. He admitted to a crisis of confidence. 'After the last game I said "I've done everything I can and we haven't had the results. I'm questioning everything …"'

On 8 February the battered side left Nairobi for an ICC Intercontinental Cup group game against the UAE. Matches in the I-Cup, which Ireland had won in 2005, are played over four days. In the amateur leagues of the Associate nations 50 over games are the norm so the ICC set up this competition to give players experience of 'time' cricket. The format allows batsmen and bowlers to build innings and bowl long spells, and could be a valuable bridge if the major nations allow Associates to compete in their domestic competitions.

Initally when Ireland were planning their winter activities, the game in Abu Dhabi was way down the list of priorities, almost an irritation. Ireland were behind in the race for a place in the final which Scotland were expected to clinch when they played UAE in Sharjah in mid-January. Although Scotland won points for a first innings lead, the Arabs surprised everyone by scoring 348 and 356-8. Scotland struggled to escape with a draw which then meant that an Irish victory would see

Birrell's team through to the final against Canada.

The four-day game began in Abu Dhabi on Saturday, 10 February. On a fabulous batting track and with a quick outfield Ireland were delighted to get the chance to bat first, and even more so when they finished the first day with 461-2. That was just one run behind Ireland's highest ever innings, set in 1893. Bray (82) and Porterfield (46) put on 122 for the first wicket, but it was not until Eoin Morgan and Andre Botha came together that Ireland began to pile on the runs. The pair were unbeaten with an Irish record stand of 325 at the end of day one, with Morgan on 182 and Botha 136.

Nobody had ever scored a double century for Ireland – Ivan Anderson made an unbeaten 198 in Canada in 1973 – but both men felt they had a chance of setting a new mark. 'I knew all about the record from the night before', said Morgan. 'It was Johnny Mooney's birthday and we had a team night out ten-pin bowling, so that got it out of my mind. The whole day and night wore me out and I slept really well so I was raring to go the next morning.' Trent Johnston was a little bruised after the ten-pin bowling, having struggled on his first encounter with the sport. 'I sent down my first delivery but the floor was like ice and I went up in the air. My arms and legs went everywhere before I fell, painfully, on the backside. The guys laughing made it worse, but I was quite happy to notice I had made a strike.'

Botha perished early on the second morning for 157 (after extending the record partnership to 360) but Morgan marched relentlessly on. After a few flutters in the nervous one-hundred-and-nineties – 'I wasn't too confident, in fact I was quite shaky but I eventually got one to put away' – he passed Anderson's record by tucking a single around the corner and reached the double century with a classic late cut. He ended his innings unbeaten on 209, having faced 238 balls and hit 24 fours and 1 six. Some were surprised that Johnston declared on 531-5, reckoning that a total of 600 or even 700 would be needed to ensure victory, but the captain explained his thinking: 'Eoin thoroughly deserves to be the record holder. We were going to bat on for a further 15 minutes but I could only see him getting out slogging and he didn't deserve that. So we pulled out early. The kid is class… the World Cup should be a great stage for him.'

The Irish bowlers were happy to have such a large target to defend as there had been plenty of criticism directed their way since Kenya. Opening bowlers Johnston and Langford-Smith had poor tournaments (they took one wicket each in the four games they played and between them conceded 339 runs) and were keen to get back on track, but the pitch they had to bowl on was clearly hugely in favour of batsmen. Although several UAE batsmen started well, a dogged Irish attack chipped away. Botha had a stomach upset which kept him off the field for more than 50 overs but he returned to take two vital wickets. With McCallan in fine form UAE were reduced to 222-9 by the close, Johnston snapping up two late scalps. Although he only picked up one wicket, Boyd Rankin was impressive and with figures of 10-1-34-1 began to enter the reckoning as a possible starter in Jamaica. 'Boyd didn't get the rewards he deserved', said Johnston, 'He bowled fantastically well. On a very flat wicket he got the ball coming through at a good pace and height and had the batsmen jumping everywhere.'

The captain mopped up the tail the following morning and, enforcing the follow-on, knocked the UAE top three batsmen over with the total on 12. Rankin returned to terrify the tail enders and ended with 4-56 as UAE were dismissed for 118 in just 48 overs. Birrell was delighted with his rookie's performance: 'Rankin's a different type of bowler. He gets steep bounce, showed in this match what he is capable of and I'm sure it will be huge for his confidence. It was fantastic to see a young guy step up to the plate when we needed him.' The coach was also relieved to win after the Kenya debacle: 'It was a flat track and the bowlers must take credit for bowling them out twice inside two days. Morgan is a class above anyone else and he showed it here. Scored at a fantastic rate, dominated the bowlers and never looked like getting out. He probably could have made 600.' Finishing the game with a day to spare was a bonus for the golfers in the side who got to experience the delights of the game on the fringes of the desert.

There was just sixteen days at home to reacquaint themselves with their families, do the laundry and get ready for the task ahead. The full-time training schedule was maintained, with weekdays spent in North County and the northern players driving up and down each day. Knox's programme intensified, with more circuit work and cardio exercises. The players racked up many miles of running in their legs and jumping exercises were increased too. The public interest and media attention also stepped up a gear, with local newspapers increasing space and overseas publications starting to take an interest in the team. The younger members of the squad enjoyed the visit of two local rock stars, Neil Hannon of the Divine Comedy and Thomas Walsh of Pugwash, which led to a full page spread in *Hot Press* magazine. RTÉ filmed reports and interviews as the significance of the impending event began to hit home with the non-cricket media.

The players helped organise their playing kit, with the ICU delivering them a giant-sized kitbag with five playing shirts, five training shirts, two pairs of shorts and a smart Magee suit and ties (the manufacturers tore up the bill in delight after the victory over Pakistan). The players had organised a golf day before Christmas to help raise funds and used their sponsorship from Kukri to pay for two extra playing shirts – swapping with their opponents would leave them with wonderful souvenirs. Kyle McCallan's job was to find fifteen pairs of shoes for formal wear, and he eventually completed his task by trawling the Next chain north and south. Big Boyd Rankin's size fifteens couldn't be accommodated by the store however, but he found a cobbler who could match the style.

There was a memorable break from routine – and a chance to wear the new suits – when President Mary McAleese invited the players, officials and their families to her official residence Áras an Uachtaráin. Before independence, the Áras was the Vice-Regal Lodge, residence of Britain's viceroy. Several of its occupants played important roles in the development of Irish cricket, from the first recorded game on the Earl of Westmoreland's front lawn in 1792. The Earl of Carlisle was a huge supporter of the game and hired Charles Lawrence to create a cricket ground in the Vice-regal lodge in 1855. Another viceroy, the Earl of Cadogan, persuaded the former England captain, Dubliner Timothy O'Brien, to get up a team to tour England in 1902. Cadogan sponsored the four matches, which gave Ireland its first taste of first-class cricket. The cricket ground fell into disuse and is now a flowerbed, and few presidents since independence have shown an interest in the sport. Eamon de Valera is reputed to have played it as a boy, but as a game it was incompatible with Dev's vision of a Celtic Ireland. During World War II he visited College Park to meet Sir John Maffey, the British ambassador who was a keen cricketer – Maffey's XI were regulars in the Trinity ground for several years. Strolling around the ground with the diplomat, de Valera picked up a discarded bat and proceeded to play a few shots in the air. However, the arrival of a press photographer horrified the taoiseach and he quickly threw the bat aside. Pictures of the Long Fellow wielding the willow would not have been good for his image.

President Mary Robinson's son, William, played for several seasons with Phoenix when his mother was in residence across Chesterfield Avenue, but it was a surprise when her successor admitted that she had some recent experience of the game. President McAleese told the Irish team that her daughter – at school in England – had taken up the game and enjoyed it immensely. She wished them well and said she was sure they would do their country proud. She was also full of praise for their efforts over the past few years and was heartened that the ICU oversaw teams that won the European Championship at six age groups in 2006. Johnston thanked the president for her generous hospitality and said how excited the team were to be in such a prestigious location. 'It was a lovely day,' Kyle McCallan said afterwards, while Trent Johnston said McAleese was 'a warm and friendly lady'. McCallan revealed that the

President seemed interested in whether we could get tickets for the historic Croke Park match against England the following weekend. 'She had a long chat with Andy White about the rugby', he said.

Although his eyes were firmly focused on the challenges ahead, Adrian Birrell knew that his annual address to the AGM of the Irish Cricket Union on Sunday, 22 February would be his last as coach. The Ballymascanlon House Hotel near Dundalk had played host to the union for decades due to its position half way between the two largest centres of Dublin and Belfast. The coach explained that the tournament in Nairobi had been heart-breaking, 'but I could not have asked for more from the team and, to bounce back the way they did in the UAE was one of the highlights of my rewarding five years as Ireland coach.' He added: 'I have had twenty years as a team coach and last year's C&G and Nairobi were the only two times I did not achieve my goals. But the fact that Ireland is now expected to win every match they play in, at their own level, shows how far we have come. We are now accepted as the best Associate team and that is the best compliment you can give me. We go to the World Cup where we will play with a smile on our faces and do ourselves justice.' The coach received an emotional standing ovation from the grateful administrators.

Little was left to chance ahead of the tournament. Robin Walsh, a former controller of BBC Northern Ireland, gave the squad a media briefing in Belfast, explaining the pitfalls that might occur and taping short interviews with those unused to close scrutiny. He discussed the issue of the Mugabe regime in Zimbabwe – which was to rear its head briefly – and suggested a way the players might answer likely questions without getting themselves or the union into trouble. The team got to face the local press at the Dublin offices of their main sponsor, Bank of Ireland. The players and management mingled with reporters and sharpened their interviewing techniques ahead of what would become an intense worldwide scrutiny over the next two months. Johnston, Birrell, new ICU chief executive Warren Deutrom and Tom Hayes of the sponsors all spoke about their hopes and dreams for what was to take place in Jamaica.

The players all piled into cars and drove north to Belfast for a similar gathering and similar sentiments. An arduous day was completed by a drive home for the Dublin players, with the O'Briens and Johnston dropping off to support a cricket book launch in Railway Union. They arrived just seconds too late to hear an extraordinary and amusing speech by the Pakistani ambassador, Toheer Ahmad, who suggested that Pakistan had 'thrown' the 1999 World Cup game against Bangladesh and might be open to a similar deal with Ireland. His quip was greeted with laughter and a suggestion from the book's co-author, James Fitzgerald, that the ICC anti-corruption unit might have something to say about that.

4 PLAYING WITH THE BIG BOYS

They laughed at me! There I was in Dublin airport, struggling with my luggage, and my team mates were laughing at me because I had three bags. 'Just you wait,' I told them, 'I've packed for seven weeks, not three!'

It was 1 March 2007 and the team was leaving Dublin for Gatwick. Vanessa, Claudia and Charlie didn't come to the airport, as I hate goodbyes. And it wasn't too bad as I knew I'd see them in Jamaica in a week or so. The following day we left Gatwick for Antigua, it was a rare chance to travel business class. The guys lapped up the luxury. I sat next to Peter Gillespie and a glass or two of champagne was consumed – but only when we checked that the coach had gone to sleep. After a seven-hour flight we landed in Antigua, but then had to fly on to Barbados before we reached our final destination of Trinidad and Tobago. The ICC had organised a warm-up programme for the week before the competition and we were assigned to Trinidad where we would play South Africa and Canada. When the fixtures were made first they had actually pitted us against Pakistan, presumably forgetting that we were playing them in the competition. It took them a few weeks to fix that one.

As we were greeted at the airport it was as if the Australian team had just landed, not Ireland. We were delighted to be rushed to the front of the queue and given a police escort to the hotel – an ambulance even followed the party, which wasn't such a bad idea when we saw the way our driver was motoring. We settled into our hotel, and discovered that one of the pleasures of playing with the big boys was that we got a room of our own. The new arrangement was definitely more comfortable than having to share a bathroom with Jeremy Bray. We shared the hotel with Pakistan, Canada and South Africa and it was a bit daunting at first bumping into world-famous stars like Shaun Pollock, Jacques Kallis and Inzamam ul-Haq over breakfast, but you soon get over that. We had two days acclimatising and practising before the first warm-up game against South Africa. Adi turned up the intensity to one hundred per cent for our practice, just the way he likes it.

The warm-up games were held in the University of West Indies in St Augustine, not far from the capital. We played South Africa on the Monday on a beautiful 35ºC day that reminded me of Australia. As usual I lost the toss and South Africa opted to bat on a fairly good wicket. What unfolded over the next 35 overs was mind-blowing stuff and at times I had to pinch myself to check that it was happening.

With three world-class deliveries Dave Langford-Smith removed their skipper Graeme Smith for 9, AB De Villiers for 5 and Kallis for 12, leaving South Africa on 42-3. Big Boyd bowled five good overs, at times worrying the far more experienced batsmen. I then came on to replace him and went for eight from my first over, not a great start, but the next four overs were possibly the best I have bowled for Ireland! Herschelle Gibbs tried to sweep me and I bowled him for 21; I had Ashwell Prince caught by Botha at slip for 7; Pollock was caught behind for 1 from a ball that left him; and I bowled Loots Bosman for 0 with a ball that jagged back. South Africa, ranked number one in the One Day International rankings and Ireland, the so-called minnows, had them on the rack at 66 for seven! Their wicketkeeper, Mark Boucher, and all-rounder Adam Hall batted well, but when Johnny Mooney dismissed Boucher with the score at 91 for eight, I remember thinking, 'Bloody hell is this happening – or am I dreaming?'

I took John off and brought myself back on to try and get the last two wickets. It didn't happen, however, and Hall (who has a test match hundred to his name) and Robin Petersen rallied, like champion players do. South Africa managed to get 192, with Andre taking the last two wickets for match figures of 2-24 off 9 overs – a fine performance against his native country. Even though we didn't finish the job off, our bowling towards the end – the so-called 'death bowling' – was top class, and a huge improvement on the way we had played in Kenya.

During the break we asked ourselves could we cause the first big upset of the World Cup before it had even started? But when you consider that their bowlers had played nearly 800 ODIs between them, our target seemed as high as Mount Everest. They came at us from the off – Jeremy was struck on the pad three times in the first over from Pollock. Adi was watching from the dressing room saying, 'God's sake Brayso get a stride in man, get a stride in'. This was one game that Adi really wanted to win.

But JB fell in the next over to Andre Nel, and Eoin went in next. 'Moggy' had been fielding down in front of the local supporters, the famous 'Trini Posse', and had clearly won them over. There were only around 1,500 people in the ground, but it seemed like 15,000. I have never heard a crowd cheer so loudly when a player got off the mark – it was a truly moving experience. We formed steady partnerships but kept losing wickets until Kevin and Andre came together. Andre cut everything through point until that hole was filled by three fielders – and still he managed to find the gap. He was eventually out to a suspect decision and that marked the beginning of the end. Charl Langeveldt and Hall, two of the best death bowlers in the world, proceeded to rip through our normally strong and reliable middle-to-lower order. The pair reeled off in-swinging yorkers which, at 140kph, were almost unplayable. Our last six wickets fell for just 18 runs and we were bundled out for 157.

So much for dreams, but we could still hold our heads up high. We had competed with the number one team in the world for most of the game. Andrew Hall was the difference between the sides, and what a class act he is. I walked into the press conference after the game proud of my squad and what we had achieved. There I met the legendary West Indian fast bowler, Colin Croft, for the first time. The giant Guyanese is now a journalist and a wonderful character. I knew from that evening that we had Crofty in our corner blowing our trumpet and proclaiming Ireland as a team to watch. He was a useful advocate when some of the commentators were querying our right to be there. I was honoured to present him with one of my Ireland shirts for his famous collection towards the end of the competition – and delighted that he left a bottle of 1919 rum for me in the hotel. He is a gentleman of the game.

We then spent thirty minutes in the South African changing room. I took the time speaking to Andre Nel, who is a true animal as soon as he crosses the rope but a bloody nice guy off it, and only too happy to part with some advice for the Irish. I also started my memorabilia collection – I had brought a few bats out with me to get signed by the teams we met and another to be signed by the sixteen captains. I have a dream that someday we will have a pool room in our home and these bats will take pride of place along the wall. The South Africans were happy to oblige and I had bat number one in the bag.

We played Canada three days later and brought in Kenny Carroll and Peter Gillespie for Will Porterfield and Kevin O'Brien. We were still a bit sore after losing to them in Nairobi, and my mood wasn't improved by losing another toss, this time to John Davison, another Aussie captaining his adopted country and then a current player with Mosman in Sydney. I played against 'Davo' for NSW against Victoria but never played with him at the club. He's an incredible hitter who held the World Cup record for fastest century (67 balls against West Indies in 2003). Against us he opted to bat but Langford-Smith continued his good form with four wickets. We had the Canadians in roughly the same place as we had the Proteas – 94 for seven – so there was a small doubt we would let it slip again. I had promised Davo at Warwick Adlam's wedding that I would get his wicket every time I played him and was overjoyed to claim it. I had set us a target of dismissing them for less than 120 and when Kyle reeled off five maiden overs and nicked two wickets we got them out for 115. The chase did not get off to a great start with Kenny dismissed for 1, but JB stuck it out and finished unbeaten on 41, with Eoin, Andre and Niall getting some much-needed time in the middle.

We weren't fully satisfied with the way we had played so we did a fitness and fielding session together for an hour, finishing off with a game of touch rugby. The squad divided along age lines, the Youngies (the eight twenty-somethings) versus the Oldies (the seven players over thirty, plus physio Knoxy). This was the start of a fierce competition which kept us amused throughout our remaining time in the Caribbean. But enough of the rugby, we were off to Jamaica.

The Jamaicans had built a new stadium for this tournament – and didn't play a single competitive match in it! But the new stadium at Trelawney, a suburb of Montego Bay on the far west of the island, did have one important role to play as it got to host the opening ceremony.

We arrived at the Holiday Inn, Sunspree Resort, early in the afternoon and had a meeting with the management. The guys' ears perked up when they heard the words 'all inclusive' – for an extra US$40 a day you could eat and drink for free. I have never seen so many of my team mates line up to pay money at a reception desk.

Bangladesh and Ireland were the only two teams staying at the resort, as the remaining fourteen were getting the five-star treatment up the road at the Ritz Carlton. There were no training facilities at the Holiday Inn so we did what we could to keep our fitness levels up, with water sports and especially tennis the main things on our menu. Peter, John, Paul and I had what you might call an 'epic battle' on centre court which was among the funniest two hours I had spent so far on tour. There were drop shots, cross-court winners, aces, air swings, tantrums, the whole lot. Paul and I eventually came out on top.

The bowlers kept in focus with some skills work with our coach-in-waiting Phil Simmons. When Adi announced his intention to quit back at the end of the 2006 season the ICU advertised the job. Phil, who played 26 tests and 201 ODIs for the West Indies, and also coached Zimbabwe, was the stand-out candidate. He was due to take over from Adi once our World Cup dream was over, but spent several weeks more than he expected with us learning about his future team and giving us the benefit of his experience. In Trelawney he taped-up a couple of tennis balls, a useful exercise for bowlers having problems controlling the way the ball swings.

On Saturday night we went along to the Ritz Carlton where the Prime Minister, Portia Simpson-Miller, had invited all the teams to a Jamaican Night. Often players dread these types of functions as they can be boring and generally go on far longer than you are promised. However, as soon as free food and drink was mentioned the bus filled up rapidly. It was a good chance for me to catch up with some old friends and I spent most of the night talking to members of the Australian team, hearing the news from Sydney from Brad Haddin, Stuart Clark and Adam Gilchrist. I also bumped into David Moore from Wollongong, who was there as the assistant coach of the West Indies. As I went to get on the bus to leave I turned to Steve Bernard, the Australian team manager, and said, 'See you in the Super Eights Steve'. He replied, 'I hope you're right Trent.'

The opening ceremony was scheduled for Sunday night and as the day was full of meetings, we kicked off with an early fitness/skills session. I had to leave early for a captains, coaches and managers meeting at the Ritz Carlton, which was the perfect chance to get my bat autographed by all my fellow skippers. The meeting went on for over an hour as we were addressed on subjects such as rule changes, logistics, the opening ceremony, media commitments, sponsors etc. I confess I left the meeting a little star struck with Ricky Ponting (Australia), Stephen Fleming (New Zealand), Rahul Dravid (India) and the rest all signing my bat and wishing Ireland the best. I got back to the hotel just as our training session finished – what a shame!

Before we headed to the opening ceremony, we had to stop off at the Ritz Carlton to have our photograph taken with the other fifteen teams. It was an unbelievable feeling standing next to absolute legends of the game, whose names and deeds will be still remembered hundreds of years from now: Sachin Tendulkar, Muttiah Muralitharan, Brian Lara. After the group shot, the sixteen captains moved to the beach for a special series of photos with the World Cup trophy.

After the photographers were finished we moved on to Trelawney Stadium. Opening ceremonies can be a bit of a bore but that was quite a showpiece. It was our first sight of the 'Blarney Army' and to see hundreds of Irish supporters in the crowd was something I will never forget. There was a bit of bother backstage when the West Indies squad, managed by the great Clive Lloyd, nearly got up and left before the ceremony even started. The host nation had not been allocated seating with the rest of the teams and had to sit down the back – not a great start by the organisers.

The teams marched out in alphabetical order, so Australia led the teams into the stadium. We walked out behind England and I could feel the butterflies flapping away. As part of the Unite for Children, Unite against AIDS awareness programme that the ICC supported throughout the competition, I walked out holding the hand of a young boy. The poor little lad was shaking and sweating – or was that just me? The organisers had got our emblem wrong too, putting the tricolour of the Republic on the placard instead of the ICU's shamrock emblem. Cricket is an all-Ireland sport and draws people from all classes and creeds, so we adopt a neutral but inspiring logo. It really baffles me that the tournament organising committee could get such things wrong.

We got an enormous cheer from the crowd – I'd say only the cheer for West Indies was bigger. Brian Lara read the players' oath and then the ninth Cricket World Cup was opened by one of the giants of the game, Sir Garfield Sobers, who once scored 365 not out in a test match and is widely regarded as the greatest all-rounder of the twentieth century. Once the teams walked off, the night came alive with a cast of more than 2,000 dancers and musicians. The fireworks lit up the sky and the entertainment was spectacular. They even ensured that there was Irish dancing and music, courtesy of a folk-rock London Irish band called the Duffys. Once the official part of the night was over we relaxed. I sat down next to one of our Close Protection Officers, 'Big D' (Sergeant Donaldson) of the Jamaican Constabulary – and had a couple of Pepsis. At least that's what it said on the cup.

A highlight of the evening was hearing the tribute to the Jamaican legend, Bob Marley, sung by his former backing singers, the I-Threes, who included Marley's wife Rita. They sang such classics as *No Woman, No Cry, I Shot the Sheriff* and *One Love* in his memory. The show closed with a hologram of Marley singing with the band, which looked for all the world like he had returned to earth. We left shortly after that to beat the traffic, and the only regret I had as we drove back was that our game against Zimbabwe wasn't the next day as the boys were looking really pumped.

It was only a thirty-five minute flight into Kingston next morning, but it was a huge journey for our team. We had heard that the city was a bit rough and ready, but the first impression was of arriving in a city with a lot of history. I thought about all the great players that came out of Jamaica, and the great musicians like Bob Marley. We had a certain amount of trepidation too, but to finally arrive there was hugely exciting. We realised we were on the big stage when we saw our motorcade from the airport. Out front were the police bikes leading our bus, and a spare bus followed us, in case ours broke down, and following that was an ambulance and a police car.

Security was a big preoccupation of the organisers, even before the tragic events that were to engulf our second week in the city. We were assigned one Close Protection Officer, or CPO, as well as three or four police officers, and we couldn't leave the hotel unless we were with

Frank or the officers. Frank was with us from the moment we arrived in Trinidad to the moment the last Irish foot hit the stairs onto the plane home in Barbados, ten weeks later. They had to know where everyone was going and who was staying behind at the hotel. They would go everywhere with us and if there was a group of five or six going out they would send two officers along. Besides for official outings and cricket activities, the only time we left the Pegasus Hotel was to go to Cuddyz sports bar, owned by the former West Indian fast bowler, Courtney Walsh. Even though we had some local knowledge – and muscle! – in Phil Simmons, and the trip was a little over a mile, we were told it just wasn't safe enough to go on our own. That said, we never got any hassle at all, just people being friendly and wishing us luck in the competition. There was one rough nut who tried to sell us some sweet-smelling herbs, but we gave him a wide berth.

Having spent nearly two years waiting for the moment we would arrive in Kingston, we wasted no time getting out of there! About ten of the guys organised a bus to take us to Ocho Rios, where our families and friends were staying. It was our first encounter with Jamaican traffic, which makes the M50 seem smooth flowing. We didn't have a police escort, but Big D came along and I sat up front with him. The driver was going nowhere in the traffic so Big D showed him his badge and said, 'I'm a police officer, you drive this thing any way it takes to get us out of here. I don't care which side of the road you drive on … ' And the driver took him at his word. The guys sat back and gripped the seats, as the driver took us down the wrong side of the road, weaving between oncoming traffic, beeping horns, chicaning along footpaths. It was truly terrifying.

We stayed in Ocho Rios till about 8.00pm, most of which I spent with Charlie and Claudia in the hotel pool. It was also good to catch up with my cousin, Debbie, who lived with us in Clontarf and played for the women's team there. My parents had spent almost three days travelling from Australia to get to Jamaica and were due to stay in Ochos Rios for a

Above: The Johnston family back in Australia. Sister Tracey, dad Trevor, Great Aunty Mabs, Trent and his mother, Anne.

Below: On the flight from London to the Caribbean, Peter Gillespie and Trent enjoy the business class fare.

Left: Dave Langford-Smith pats Jeremy Bray on the back as he leaves the field after scoring 115 not out against Zimbabwe in the opening World Cup match at Sabina Park.

Below: Paul McGann, Brendan and Camilla O'Brien and Brendan Carroll show the colours in Kingston.

Above: Eoin Morgan, Niall O'Brien, Will Porterfield, Andrew White and Kevin O'Brien celebrate capturing the final Zimbabwe wicket to secure the tie.

Below: Fans on the party mound; back row: David Hall, John O'Donoghue, Niall Sheehy and Dermot Cribbin; front row: Rosa Werli, Liz Sheenan and James McElvenna.

Above: Kevin O'Brien runs to congratulate Trent Johnston on holding a vital catch against Pakistan. In taking the catch he had damaged his shoulder again.

Left: Andre Botha and Niall O'Brien celebrate capturing the crucial wicket of the Pakistan captain Inzaman ul-Haq.

Above: Bob Woolmer and Inzaman ul-Haq leave the field after the defeat.

Below: Dave Langford-Smith goes front and centre to lead the celebrations after beating Pakistan. The captain and coach were off talking to the world's media.

Above: Trent Johnston with his mother, Anne, Claudia and Charlie in Sabina Park.

Below: Eoin Morgan with the M16 gun outside the Cara Lodge in Georgetown, Guyana. The policeman who lent him the weapon got in hot water after this photograph appeared in the newspapers.

It was a bit hot in Guyana to get dressed for net practice.

Left: Eoin Morgan leads the 'Youngies' in the Snip du Jour Rugby Cup which kept the squad amused throughout the tournament.

Right: Iain Knox working on Kevin O'Brien. The physio earned his corn on the trip, not least for the work on the captain's shoulder.

fortnight. I hadn't seen my father for almost two years, so it was fantastic that he had been able to make it. All my family had been in Ireland for the qualifiers in 2005, so Mum and Dad already knew many of the Irish supporters staying at the Sunset Grande. They immediately slotted in to 'Blarney Army' mode.

Training next morning was a short distance away at Kensington CC and it was a short, easy session. About ten of the team went on to Sabina to watch the World Cup's opening game, West Indies v Pakistan, and to get a feel for the atmosphere. We were told by the ICC not to wear team gear or colours, so as not to take away from the main event on the pitch, but we were spotted anyway and appeared on the TV and big screen a few times. It was good to relax and see what it was about. There were a few Irish fans there that day so it was good to meet some old friends.

On Wednesday we had a rare lie-in before getting our first run out on Sabina Park in the afternoon. It wasn't too intensive, maybe five overs each for the bowlers, and we let the net bowlers (local club players who come along to provide cannon fodder for the batsmen), take the strain. When I'm at home I'm usually very quiet the night before a game, but I was a bit more relaxed here. We had a team meeting to talk about the game and work out some tactics and approaches, and afterwards a few of us went up to Cuddyz bar for a bite. I enjoy having a beer the night before a game, but in the World Cup I toned it down big time. Still, I did have a couple with Jeremy, while the rest of the guys stayed on water.

I watched TV through to midnight, drinking lots of liquids to guard against cramp the next day. Most nights before a game I'd have a line of bottles beside the bed – before Zimbabwe I drank two litres of water and two litres of Gatorade throughout the night. Knoxy reckoned that the bowlers would lose three to five litres playing in that heat – so you have to have that and more on board before you start. I didn't sleep too well because I was up for a pee every hour, plus there were a few nerves jangling inside too. Another problem was the band playing across the road in Redemption Park – as was the case on the nights before all our games. The music was so loud you'd hear it with the doors, shutters, windows and curtains closed.

I was up early and straight down for breakfast. I'm not a great eater before games, maybe just a plate of fruit and a glass of watered-down orange juice. We're all different, of course, and I had to watch Jeremy Bray tuck into salt fish, a grill, toast, fruit and lots of juice. We haven't reached the level where we get scientific advice on our diets, but I'd listen to what the big boys say about it. I remember talking to the Australia batsman, Michael Bevan, who studied his scores and found that if he didn't have dairy products for two days before a game he would go out and perform better. The difference was phenomenal – 100-200% – and he worked out it was something to do with his eyes and the speed of how he would pick up the ball.

Cricket is the only game in the world with meals actually written into the laws, but the life of a bowler isn't easy, and I'd skip lunch if we have to bowl after the break. The result is that I can go all day without a meal, which isn't good for the system. I wouldn't recommend this approach to young players – but it has been my routine for so long I just couldn't change it. I do make sure that I consume plenty of sports drinks and water, and I've recently started eating bananas during the game too, which seems to help.

Because play started at 9.30am (its usually 10.45am or 11.00am at home) we left for the ground at 7.35am. We were supposed to meet at 7.30am, but Peter 'Polish' Gillespie usually shows up a spilt second before 7.30. I don't know if he does it to wind us up, but he's generally last on the bus. The Mooney boys look like they've spent the night on the couch and have had no sleep at all. We usually operate a fines system with a penalty for time keeping but decided to drop it on this tour. Thankfully, the only time anyone was late was Mooners on the day we left Jamaica, because he'd had a skinful the night before.

Aboard the bus the guys tend to keep to themselves and listen to their iPods. I always listen to Paddy Casey's 'Living' album, but it's the only time I ever listen to him. A few of those songs really get me and its part of my routine now. The rest are all there doing their own thing – Kenny Carroll listens to U2 and 50 Cent, Kevin O'Brien mostly rap. Dave Langford-Smith has very modern tastes, with his iPod bursting with the likes of Snow Patrol, David Kitt, Sufjan Stevens, Radiohead and Powderfinger. Kyle McCallan is another creature of habit and always turns to *Belfast Child* by Simple Minds as we get near the ground. Peter and Paul also asked the driver, Llaurence, to play the CD of Martin Byrne's anthem *Come on Ireland*, and after a couple of plays we all sang along with it. Kingston was warm and balmy that day, and the early start reminded me of Australia. It was very hot, but I've played in worse. Brett Lee told me about a test Australia played in Sharjah when Pakistan was using that country for home games during the Afghan war. The heat was so intense that Brett – one of the fittest men in the game – would bowl two overs, go off for an ice bath and then come back. Vanessa played a bit of cricket in Australia, when we first went there, and passed out twice due to the intense heat.

Zimbabwe must have left their kit in the dressing room overnight because they were already set up in the room we were supposed to have. We didn't mind at all, as we knew we would be the 'away' team for the final two games, and it allowed us to get used to the same room for what would be home for ten or eleven hours each day. The rooms were enormous, with lots of room for personal space. I got in first, and grabbed a nice spot in the corner, near the door, which is a must as captain as there's always people coming in to talk to you. If I don't know the umpires I'd always find out where their rooms are and go up and introduce myself, so that day I called up to see Barry Jerling of South Africa and Englishman Ian Gould.

My dressing room routine is to get all my kit out of my bag and hang it up. Everything goes in the cupboard and when I have the hats and caps up I'm ready to rock and roll. Andy White has a similar routine, while Moggy pulls everything out onto the floor and sorts through it all. Niall brings five bats in a separate bag and he lines them up and plays with them before selecting his chosen one for the day. Brayso's routine seems to revolve around the loo, which he visits dozens of times before the start. It's quite a chilled time and Peter Gillespie would rig up his iPod speakers and look after the sounds. With seventy-five minutes to go before the start, Adi stepped up and had a chat and I said something brief about what we needed to do before we took off for warm ups.

The captain has one really important job to do before a game – which is to take part in the ceremony that decides who chooses to bat and bowl. I would always ask Roy Torrens to give me a shout about 8.45, when I'd slip away to have a shower and a bit of 'me' time before donning the match kit. We were briefed in Montego Bay about the protocol of the toss and how the TV people would be running the show. It's a strange little ceremony which can often be the most important moment of the day. The so-called 'luck' of the Irish saw me win two out of eight tosses – and they were the two games we won.

I played in a couple of games in Australia that were televised, but the only TV game I had captained in was Ireland's game against Hampshire in 2006. The home captain always brings out the coin, but I wasn't sure if I had to bring one in those circumstances. I slipped one in my pocket just in case. Sure enough the Sky commentator chirped up with 'here's Trent Johnston the Irish captain. Hope you've got a coin Trent.' That could have been a bit embarrassing on live TV. Against Zimbabwe I remembered that incident so I had a coin ready, but the match referee, Roshan Mahanama, had one too and I let him use his. We had a chat with the commentator, tossed, chatted again and off we went. That day was funny because we had decided to bat first, having seen how the wicket played two days before for West Indies. But, although I lost the toss, Zimbabwe captain Prosper Utseya asked us to bat anyway.

9.25am ticked past and off to the middle strode Jeremy and William to warm applause from the supporters. The umpires delayed for a minute to make sure they started at precisely 9.30am, and Will took the first ball of the first game of Ireland's first World Cup. A straight bat pushed the ball out to mid-on as the other thirteen of us lined across the balcony. I confess my thoughts were elsewhere, as I was a bit worried that Vanessa and the children and my parents hadn't yet arrived. I spotted Kyle and Andy's parents in the stand next to our dressing rooms and I knew all the families were seated together – but there was no sign of mine. I was thinking 'What's going on, where are they?' I was worried because I was sure Vanessa and Mum would have been on the first bus out of Ocho Rios to be there in good time.

Once they showed up I was happier and I enjoyed watching the guys put a few runs together. The rest of the team, who were sitting on the balcony, seemed like they'd walked into a sweet shop as they looked around the stadium with eyes stretched wide, reading the banners from Strabane to Railway Union. Our joy was ended on the sixth ball of the first over, when Porty edged the ball to slip, via the keeper. But we were quickly cheered as Jeremy found his feet. Zimbabwe obviously hadn't done their homework on him because they kept feeding his best shot and he kept hitting it for four and six. Anything wide of off stump he throws the kitchen sink at and they bowled poorly to him. After this game the big boys worked him out instantly, they didn't even need a video system to identify his weakness. In his defence it still took bowlers of the calibre of Glenn McGrath, Shane Bond, Shaun Pollock and Mohammed Sami, to actually dismiss him. But it bemused me the way Zimbabwe bowled to him. Wordsworth has been my roommate for the last three years and is my best mate in Ireland. We've known each other since we were twelve years old and he has not stopped whingeing during that whole period. He has been the most prolific scorer of runs domestically, and for Ireland since his arrival from Australia, and it was fitting that he scored Ireland's first ODI hundred against Scotland, and first in a World Cup against Zimbabwe. Jeremy will surely go down as one of Ireland's greatest opening batsmen. The 115 he made was a huge effort for him in the heat, and to remain unbeaten through the fifty overs was a great feat of stamina and concentration. He became only the twelfth batsman to bat through the full overs of a World Cup innings, joining such greats as Sunil Gavaskar (India), Glenn Turner (New Zealand) and Geoff Marsh (Australia). On his way off he was grabbed by the TV inquisitors and asked how he felt. What did they expect him to say? Sure enough he gave them an, 'It feels pretty good, mate', before running up the steps to a huge welcome from his team mates.

The ball had been swinging early on and the Zimbabweans had Niall, Moggy and Andre in trouble, but Andrew and I stuck around with Brayso and got twenties ourselves. It was good for Andy because his place had been in doubt before the game as we weren't sure whether to play him or John Boy. In terms of batting they were equal and in fielding John was far superior, but I needed a bowler I could go to in a crisis, and Whitey was the best option. All the talk during the break was whether 221 was enough – personally I thought at the time that it was 30 or 40 too much. I really thought we could get hold of them. Boyd and Lanky had been in such good form, and seeing the way the new ball had swung – I was sure we could get among them. And I knew the way they could capitulate under the pressure of the World Cup, playing a team they should beat.

So with the momentum we had, 221 was more than enough – provided we bowled well. But we didn't bowl that well. Lanky and Boyd were nervous and both bowled a few wides, which was a recurring problem for us throughout the competition. Our fielding was excellent but we dropped a few catches early on, including Terence Duffin twice in one ridiculous Rankin over. The big fella finally picked up his first wicket off the sixth ball of that over, when Niall hung on to an edge.

We're really big on the idea of The Team as being a fifteen-man unit, and that's not just for show or to make the non-players feel better. Every one of the guys had a crucial role to play that day. Just keeping the bowlers and fielders stocked with water was vital, and Kenny, Peter and the Mooneys would regularly run around to refill the coolers positioned outside the ropes. The bowlers would drink every over, and it was important to keep the water cool for them. When a wicket fell the four would come straight out with drinks and towels. Towards the end of the Zimbabwe innings, Paul ran around with a banana for Jeremy. John, too, always had to be ready to take over if anyone needed to leave the field, but there was a rota system in place where two of the reserves stayed in the dressing room and the two others were posted on the side of the pitch. When we were batting they were just as important, keeping a spare set of gloves at pitch side in case they were needed, as well as wet towels, dry towels, and whatever drinks the particular batsman preferred. It was a vital role and should not be underestimated as they had to keep us serviced from the first to the 300th ball – or 330th given the amount of wides we bowled.

The Zimbabweans recovered from losing the early wicket to reach 94 for one, when we induced a mini collapse to 133 for five. But Stuart Matsikinyeri and wicketkeeper, Brendon Taylor, put together a good stand and withstood everything I tried to break them up. We got a bit of luck when a ball hit back to Kyle flicked his hand and broke the wicket at the non-striker's end, and the TV replay showed Taylor was out of his ground.

I went to Kyle and asked him what he thought about bringing myself and Andre back and he said, 'OK, do it'. Besides Kyle, I'd usually consult Niall and Moggy about on-field tactics. They might be young guns but they've got great cricket brains. Niall's my eyes and ears out there, he sees everything and can tell me if a fielder's angle is wrong or we need to change a position. The team came together in a huddle and I told them my new plan. We only had two overs left each, but we could turn up the heat better than anyone else. There were six overs left in the game and they only needed 15 to win. I could see a few of the guys were no longer convinced we could win, but I reminded them that we had spoken the previous night and that morning about how these guys could crumble. And the pressure we had them under was so intense that the conditions were perfect for another collapse.

I could see it in the Zimbabweans eyes that they were gone. I closely watched a lot of their series with West Indies around Christmas and knew Gary Brent could hold a bat, but if we could get him out we could get hold of the other guys. Andre and I tied them down completely over the next four overs, giving up just six runs, and Boatsy bowled a peach of a slower ball that trapped Brent in front of middle stump.

With two overs left, they needed nine runs and had three wickets in hand, and I turned to Kevin. His first ball was a rank full toss, but their captain smacked it straight to Porty. Kevin bowled like a dream and then I ran out Mpofu off the last ball of a maiden over – a maiden, in the 49th over of the game. It was unbelievable.

Still nine to win, and I turned to Andy because he was the one I reckoned would be able to bowl the ball on a 5 cent coin – but he bowled some awful rubbish that last over. First ball was a full toss hit for two, second ball was short and square cut for two, next was another full toss and Matsikinyeri spooned it to midwicket where it fell just short of Boyd, and he took a single to go off strike. So, it was four to win off three balls. Rainsford drove the fourth ball past cover and took one. Next ball, I nearly took a blinder at backward point but Matsikinyeri got two, which meant we couldn't win. And that was also the moment I reinjured my shoulder – I felt something go, but with one ball left I wasn't going anywhere.

Nine times out of ten Matsikinyeri would have hit that last ball out of the park. It was a half volley, and Whitey couldn't turn a bottle top. He just held the ball across the seam and speared it in. But Matsikinyeri swung so hard that he missed the ball – Nobby went for the stumping but the batsman had never left his crease. But then the non-striker, Rainsford, just took off and came right down the pitch towards his team mate. Nobby kept a cool head and lobbed it back to Andy, who smashed the stumps. Scores level, and a tie secured!

Their coach, Kevin Curran, looked shocked – his team had won it, lost it, won it, lost it, won it, won it, won it and finally tied. It was one point each, but Adi explained that the way the group stood, it was just as valuable as a win. One win and we'd almost certainly qualify. We set off on the first of our laps of honour and as we came down the steps, some of the guys turned left towards our families and the Party Stand. I called them back and explained that we would lap anti-clockwise, so we could finish up in front of our families. It was a marvellous circuit, and it was great to see that so many locals had taken to us at that stage. I clung onto one of the Pepsi stumps I had grabbed as a souvenir, and a few of the guys put on silly hats thrown to them by the fans. We got a huge roar from the fans in the Headley Stand and the raucous Party Stand animals, and it was nice to recognise a few of the friends we had made among the locals and ex-pats. Finally we ended up in front of our families and I was so happy to pick out Vee, Charlie, Claudia and my parents. It was a very special moment in my life.

Afterwards, I was taken down to the media centre to explain the game away to the world's press, before heading back to grab a brief moment with my family before they were whisked off to Ocho Rios. I returned to the dressing room where I discovered, to my horror, that the entire beer supply had been already drained. Thanks guys!

5 HAIL, GLORIOUS ST PATRICK

For most of the travelling fans, St Patrick's Day started in the dark, with alarm clocks and early morning calls around 5.00am. Most of the supporters based themselves on the north coast of the island in the resort of Ocho Rios. This settlement – its name means eight rivers, although there isn't even a stream to be seen in the town – depends on tourism for its living. Every weekday an American cruise liner docks offshore and spills its human cargo into the town, while modern hotels cater for US 'spring break' college students and, mostly British, package holidaymakers.

The Blarney Army moved in after the weekend of the opening ceremony, with the vast bulk of its troops based in the Sunset Grande hotel, an all-inclusive 730-room behemoth with security guards to keep the harsher realities of Jamaican life outside. The hotel's manager confided to Rangan Arulchelvan, a Railway Union player and himself a Dublin hotelier, that they may have miscalculated the Irish fans capacity for consumption – the bar was drunk dry on at least three occasions as fans pursued value from their all-in deals.

According to the guidebooks and holiday brochures, Ocho Rios to Kingston is a journey of 80km. What they don't say however, is that the road between the two is as tortuous as an epileptic rattlesnake, and just as dangerous. The Irish fans had secured various modes of transport for their journeys, which lasted between two and three hours. Luxury coaches left the Sunset Grande in a convoy, while smaller Juta buses and taxis headed nervously for the black hills above Ocho Rios.

Being St Patrick's Day – or 'JamPatrick's Day' as the locals called it – Mother Nature made an extra special effort for her visitors. The magical Fern Gully, just south of Ocho Rios, winds for three to 4km through a primeval forest filled with giant trees and 500 varieties of fern. Ireland might claim forty shades of green, but this serene valley surely doubles that tally. The gully afforded spectacular views but the travellers busily watching the roadside cliff's edges and traffic speeding towards and past them missed many of these.

One group of travellers were so unimpressed with the journey that they took the aerial route. Joseph Clinton, of The Hills cricket club in Skerries, explains: 'I was there with my wife Barbara and eighteen-month-old son, Adam, and the bus trip to the first game was very hard on him. So we hired a helicopter that took us from Ocho Rios to Kingston in twenty minutes, leaving us five minutes from the ground. We shared it with another man so it cost $250.'

The bus journey also opened many people's eyes to a Jamaica not covered in the Berlitz guide. It is a poor country, and the people who live in the inland villages have it harder than the rest of their compatriots. A hand-painted sign proudly proclaims the settlement of Ewarton as: 'home of Asafa Powell', the 100m world record holder. 'I'd say he learnt to run fast to escape the traffic', quipped one Irishman as the bus sped through the shanty village with indecent haste. The Rio Cobre gorge – known as Bog Walk – provided a useful comfort stop, while the road continued past a fast-flowing river – and across it at a terrifying bridge with no side walls – before the driver made an unscheduled halt. Checking the passengers to see whether any women were present, he announced that our trip to Jamaica wouldn't be complete without seeing what he called, 'The Rock'. This turned out to be a riverside cave hewn by nature into an extraordinary geological formation best described as 'anatomically correct'.

One busload was horrified to discover that an electricity cable had become entangled with their vehicle, and grateful that an experienced ESB employee, John Morgan, was aboard. The former Malahide batsman clambered onto the roof to clear the cable. Another group were less lucky as it took three different vehicles to get them, late, to Sabina, despite the best efforts of Greysteel and Eglinton cricketer, Tommy Mailey. As the terrain flattened out the traffic got faster. The old capital of Spanish Town flashed by as the suburbs of Kingston welcomed the visitors. There had been many warnings about the lawless state of the capital, and a group of independent travellers, Siobhán McBennett of Rush, Mary Mackey of Malahide and Elaine Coburn of Railway Union, were relieved to find a motorcycle cop when they ended up in a less salubrious *barrio*, and delighted to receive an escort to Sabina Park.

The old stadium – first used for a test match in 1930 – is itself in an area where tourists usually avoid, but the fears were to prove unfounded as the Irish fans enjoyed a trip remarkably free from crime. The supporters dispersed around the ground, most of those on the trip organised by Paul Mooney's wife, Cindy Preece, primarily the 180 members of North County cricket club, gathered in the George Headley Stand. Others discovered their seats were in the rickety temporary structure next to the old Kingston CC pavilion, while the hedonists headed for the mound – a raucous den that went by the name of 'The Party Stand'. It was here that the Blarney Army made its name as a colourful, friendly bunch who enjoyed their sport. A large amount of the credit for this must go to a man who wasn't even Irish.

Tapping into the welcoming inclusive nature of the Irish cricket zeitgeist, Australian Rules footballer, Adrian Raftery, followed his own dream to Sabina Park. He had visited Dublin and Galway in 2006 as part of the Australian Wombats veterans' squad, who played an International Rules series with their Gaelic football counterparts. That December he met a fellow Sydneysider, Kylie Davis, fell instantly in love and in January persuaded her to marry him. He also persuaded her that a wonderful honeymoon venue would be Jamaica, and that it was particularly nice in March. The following March.

Raftery brought home one important souvenir from his trip with the Wombats – a garish green leprechaun suit complete with orange beard and stovepipe hat. He had worn it to a Wombats team meeting and promised the coach John Platten, an AFL legend who was born on 17 March 1963 – that he would wear it in his honour on his next birthday. Draping his 6'5" frame in the outfit, Raftery was a striking figure in the Party Stand. The stand itself is a very Caribbean way of watching cricket – the admission charge of US$70 to 90 entitled the spectator to a lunch (jerk chicken with red beans and rice) and eight precious drink vouchers. These could be exchanged for water, Pepsi, beer or rum – although the soft drinks seemed low on the list of priorities for most fans. A huge loudspeaker was the centrepiece of the stand, with loud music interrupting the quieter moments on the field. Local reggae classics such as *One Love, Three Little Birds* and *Punky Reggae Party* were popular, but the Irish introduced a new standard to the Kingston canon.

Come on Ireland was an instant anthem, rapidly surpassing *Ireland's Call*, as a fans' favourite. It was written by Martin Byrne, a former star bowler with The Hills, in response to a call for an anthem from David O'Connor, an independent councillor on Fingal County Council and chairman of North County CC. In February O'Connor had roped in the *Fingal Independent* newspaper and local firm Murphy Environmental, who stumped up €1,000 prize money. Entries were received from far and wide, with a final strum-off at the North County pavilion in Balrothery, and Byrne's composition was a popular winner. 'The World Cup is something totally new for Irish cricket, and it was felt by many that we needed an anthem to mark the occasion, and we'll be singing the winning song in Jamaica,' said O'Connor. Two weeks later the councillor was on the plane to Montego Bay with some freshly minted CDs, one of which he presented to the Party Stand DJ. An unashamedly upbeat tune, it was a jaunty mix – surely previously unheard – of steel band and accordion. Byrne's lyrics were highly topical, nodding to other Irish sporting feats. The first verse ran:

> You can talk about Italia and Euro '88.
> With the oval ball in Croke Park the future's looking great.
> Now we're on a new adventure and things are on the up.
> We are going to Jamaica for the Cricket World Cup.
> C'mon Ireland c'mon Ireland.
> We're going to bring the World Cup back
> C'mon Ireland c'mon Ireland.
> And win or lose we're going to have the craic.
> © Martin Byrne

Had Byrne been on a pay-per-play deal, he would have been a wealthy man after the competition as the Party Stand DJ blasted out his refrain over after over.

Johnny Mooney and Ken Carroll looked out of the dressing room across to the New Stand, where four flags hung side by side: the tricolour, the union jack, the Ulster flag and a GAA flag. 'Where else would you see that except a cricket match?' asked Mooney rhetorically. Another great example of the multi-cultural nature of cricket came at the fiftieth birthday celebration of Jody Morgan, father of Eoin, in Ocho Rios. The party turned into a sing-song at which *Amhrán na bhFiann* was followed by *The Sash My Father Wore* with liberal doses of *C'mon Ireland* and *Ireland's Call*.

It was quite a gruelling day for the Irish supporters. They roared their heroes on and cheered every run or wicket, but when the tension became unbearable a strange silence descended. It was then that Raftery rose to the occasion and stoked up the support to give their all. The notion of cheerleading is pretty alien to Irish sports culture, but it was one occasion when an individual seized the moment and got the crowd going.

As Jeremy Bray flagged in the heat two days earlier against

Zimbabwe, he heard a strange sound – the old war cry of the Christian Brothers School, Lewisham, Sydney. He scanned the ground and spotted the giant leprechaun waving at him. It was then he twigged that the leprechaun was Raftery, an old school mate who used to coach his little brother Shaun. He gave him a thumbs-up. 'It was crazy to see Jezza score a ton against Zimbabwe,' recalled Raftery, 'There was a very small crowd there that day and I must admit they were very quiet at first – as if they didn't know what to do. As a many time veteran of the Sydney Cricket Ground I felt it was my duty to help out by leading the chants, songs, sledging and support for the Irish guys.' Raftery had crossed paths with Bray once since they left school. The future leprechaun had a girlfriend from County Laois and once visited her home in Raheen. On a visit to Portlaoise he spotted a cricket match going on and stopped for a chat. The locals asked him did he play for New South Wales, 'as the last Australian that came up here did'. Raftery asked who that was and was astonished to be told it was Jeremy Bray.

Another Australian, John Archer, admitted that he went without lunch at Sabina Park for two days because he was afraid he'd miss the action if he queued at the chicken stand. Archer was the headmaster of Canobolas High School in Orange, New South Wales, before his retirement. One of his former pupils was Dave Langford-Smith who he had visited in Ireland the summer before. 'We went to see him at Phoenix,' said Archer, 'but the game was washed out. So I promised him that he would go to watch him in the World Cup if he made the Irish squad.' With DLS's old biology teacher and cricket coach, Jim Finn, Archer made good his promise and was delighted to join the Irish fans in Sabina.

As the tension rose against Pakistan, the assistant coach, Matt Dwyer, walked around to the Party Stand to gee them up and demand more raucous support. Matt's brother, Willie, cut a fine figure, his curious blend of Irish and Jamaican fashions attracting much attention and his shamrock-shaped sunglasses making many newspaper front pages throughout the fortnight. Brian Robinson of Donemana was also quite eye-catching in a bikini top with Jamaican flag design. David O'Connor, dressed as St Patrick in a tricoloured tunic, was also having his photo taken frequently alongside his fellow Fingallians including Clifford Costello and Martin Russell.

Another group that received plenty of attention in *The Jamaican Gleaner* newspaper was The Terenure Walnuts. This side are regulars on the 'taverners' circuit, playing other pub teams and the likes of the Theatrical Cavaliers, Dalkey Archive and Evening Herald XIs in social games on Friday evenings. The cricket is mostly gentle, and the players a mix of enthusiastic twenty over specialists and former league players, such as Tony Connell and Brian Brennan (Civil Service), David Brennan (CYM) and Mick Fanagan (Phoenix) whose better days are captured in yellowing scorebooks. So it was quite a shock to discover that the Walnuts had secured a prime fixture against Melbourne CC as part of their Jamaican holiday. Melbourne is a historic club nestled in the foothills of the Blue Mountains that loom above Kingston, whose current president is Courtney Walsh, once the holder of the record of most wickets in test matches with 519. The Walnuts were stunned to read in the *Gleaner* the day before the game that their opponents would include no less than eight Test cricketers including Walsh, Lawrence Rowe, Nehemiah Perry and sixty-three-year-old Maurice Foster. Foster's previous encounter with an Irish side was a bit embarrassing – he was run out for two as the West Indies were bowled out for 25 at Sion Mills in 1969.

Happily for the Irishmen, they were able to convince their hosts that they were nowhere near that standard and several of their stars stayed on the sidelines. The Walnuts were given two West Indies under-nineteen players and the current Jamaica wicketkeeper Carlton Baugh to ensure something approaching parity. Club president, John Donnellan, got to open the batting against Courtney Walsh and the rest of the team, whose ages ranged from thirty-seven-year-old Darren Phillips to seventy-three-year-old Stewart Cree, mustered 135, a total their hosts passed in just 12 overs. The real highlight of the day was to come as legends Michael Holding and Viv Richards arrived and spent several hours chatting with the Dubliners. 'They couldn't have been nicer hosts,' said Phillips, 'we've invited them back to play us in Terenure College'.

In Sabina, the Ireland players' families were gathered in the newly-built Northern Stand, a five-tiered structure that includes corporate boxes, dressing rooms and media areas. The dressing rooms were perched side-by-side on top of the sightscreen with staircases leading up from the pitch. For all three games the Irish were based in the one to the left as they looked onto Sabina, with their families sitting in the area to their left. There was plenty of room to move around for the first two games, and many fans switched seats with abandon as the stewards relaxed. The fans brought the famous Irish wit into play, with adaptations of reggae classics such as *No Rankin, No Ball, Trentstown Rock* and *Uptown Boyd Rankin* sharpened in the bars of Kingston and Ocho. More quick wit was in evidence at the Ireland v West Indies game when a group of premiership footballers including Andrew Cole and Sol Campbell turned up. The fans also spotted Dwight Yorke of Sunderland, the club managed by Irishman Roy Keane. 'Does Keano know you're drinking?, Does Keano know you're drinking?' was the chant begun by John Morgan, uncle of Eoin.

The area around Sabina Park has the driest micro-climate in Kingston, but the grey and overcast day saw several showers. Tony Becca, the doyen of Jamaican cricket writers, was stunned at the colour of the wicket when he arrived at the ground. 'I have been watching cricket here for more than fifty years and I have never seen it as green. It's the groundsman's St Patrick's Day present to Ireland!'

Of course, it would have been just as much a present to Pakistan had Inzamam not called 'tails' when match referee, Chris Broad, tossed the coin at 9.00am. Trent Johnston realised how important the decision was. 'The toss was huge and I finally came to the party and won one for the lads.' In a competition where it was widely acknowledged that the toss had an enormous effect on performances, Johnston won just two of the nine tosses.

Pakistan lost wickets early and often, with Rankin's bounce discomfiting several batsmen and dismissing Younis Khan of their fabled 'Big Three' for a duck. All six bowlers took at least one wicket, with Andre Botha's figures of 8-4-5-2 being the ninth most economical spell in One Day International history (the top of this particular table is 10-8-3-4 by Phil Simmons, the man who succeeded Adrian Birrell after the World Cup). The Irish fans were delirious during the interval, daring to dream that Ireland might just score the 133 runs needed to win.

A large proportion of fans in the Party Stand came from the GAA club in the Cayman Islands, a tax haven 290km to the north-west that was part of Jamaica until 1962. Most of the eighty Irish people that came over to Sabina work in financial services on Cayman, or with the Digicel mobile phone company that has made huge inroads in the Caribbean and sponsors the West Indies team. One of the Cayman fans, a former Sligo Gaelic footballer, was to pay dearly for his ignorance of the game. During a thirty-five minute rain delay midway through the Irish innings he climbed the fence that separated the partying fans from the field of play, believing in his inebriation that Ireland had won. After a couple of sidesteps he was apprehended by security, with the PA announcer telling the stadium that he would be liable to a fine of 100,000 Jamaican dollars (about €1,100). The Sligoman's boss was in the stadium and with the Jamaican police applying a creative approach to restorative justice, secured his release. The Sabina invader and his new uniformed friends then repaired to the Irishman's hotel room where they enjoyed the rest of the game over a few beers. The fan suffered more on the following Monday when faxes of his behaviour were sent through to his office in Cayman. *The Sun* newspaper chose the headline 'Batty Boy' on the story about his foray, but that phrase carries slightly different overtones on either side of the Atlantic. While 'batty' implies stupidity in Ireland, in

Jamaica it is a term of abuse for homosexuals.

Never have dark clouds and rain been more welcome in the long, soggy history of cricket in Ireland. The delay, which came with the score at 81-4, reduced the Irish target by five precious runs, a tiny but potentially vital break as the three overs lost were likely to be irrelevant. There was very little singing as the target was neared. The light was deteriorating rapidly and Kevin O'Brien jokingly called for a torch. In darker conditions than they left the field for earlier, the umpires kept Ireland out in the middle, a situation that only benefited the Pakistanis who could win by bowling out the opposition.

Every run of the O'Brien brothers' 38 run partnership was applauded, none more than Niall's brutal six into the stands off Shoaib Malik. That shot produced a roar that caused the stadium to shake – by now the West Indian support was four square behind the Irish – but his stumping next ball was greeted with silence that could be heard all the way to the Spire in O'Connell Street. When White and McCallan were out in the following over the tension became too much for some fans, who left the arena for respite. Sixteen needed off 12 overs; five singles reduced the target before O'Brien timed a beautiful four through extra cover. Four more singles and a gifted wide took Ireland to the brink. Bob Woolmer stared down from the balcony with a face like thunder.

Kevin O'Brien fisted the air and grinned to his team mates on the balcony. On the fourth ball of the 41st over Trent Johnston clubbed the ball high into the Headley Stand and into the massed ranks of delirious Ireland supporters. He paused for a second, before leaping in the air. As he fell to earth he was swamped by his team mates. The eccentric umpire, Billy Bowden, crooked his fingers and lifted them slowly towards the stars that had just arrived to witness one of the greatest moments in the history of Irish sport.

The veteran Irish sports journalist, Con Houlihan, wrote in his *Sunday World* column that it was the most sensational result in international sport since North Korea beat Italy in the 1966 football World Cup. 'In a way it was even more sensational', he wrote: 'in soccer you can snatch a goal and hold on to it, as North Korea did; in cricket you are thoroughly assessed over a much longer period'. Houlihan wrote, 'There might be games almost as thrilling but my heart wouldn't be so deeply involved: if Kerry had been playing in the All Ireland Final, the tension couldn't be more.'

One of the witnesses was David Dunn from Derry: 'Win or lose, we were always going to enjoy it. But this is something else – bring on the West Indies'. Raymond Byrne from County Cavan lives in Jamaica: 'I have been twenty-four years out here. I'm a big Gaelic man, a big soccer man, and a big rugby man. I've never been a big cricket man but you have to be now. This supersedes the lot.'

Sri Lankan born Rangan Arulchevan, long based in Dublin, was proud of his adopted countrymen: 'Look at that performance. It was not all about the big names. It was a great day for everybody involved in Irish cricket at grassroots level – just look at the guys in that squad who started playing their cricket in the fourths at Bready, Strabane, Railway Union, etc. and how far they have come. When I was captain of the fourths at Railway, I had three of that team with me and Kevin and Kenny got their first fifties with me. I can't tell you how proud I am, and I know there are lots more like me around the country.'

Former ICU chairman, Joe Doherty from Strabane, spoke movingly about his emotions as Johnston carted the ball into the stands. 'My mind wandered back, in a surreal way, to where the journey to Jamaica began for me, as a six-year-old boy with my father and grandfather, watching Strabane play St Johnston in a league game in 1956. I know from speaking to others that many of us were having similar reflective periods. The point that was made to me, time after time, was that cricket in Ireland is a community experience, a network of 'families' welded together by a common love. It takes us to be lifted from our terrestrial and parochial rivalries to appreciate how much we have in common and that no one is any more equal than the other.'

All over their homeland new fans were being seduced by this thrilling game while in Sabina Park 2,500 believers with banners proclaiming their allegiance to Killymallaght, Railway Union, Strabane and Balbriggan were shouting themselves hoarse and looking forward to the greatest St Patrick's Night of their lives.

6 A TASTE FOR MORE

Leaving Sabina Park after the game against Zimbabwe the boys were enjoying their first taste of big time cricket – and we wanted more. The twenty-minute bus ride back to the hotel saw *Ireland's Call* sung several times and I gave my customary loud rendition of *Aru Cha Cha*. Arriving back at the team hotel and I continued what had developed into a routine of shaking hands with our security man, Big D, and he would reply 'Respect, One love'.

Sky Sports, RTÉ, Newstalk and a huge sub-continental press contingent were there: 'Can you guys win this group?', 'Is this a flash in the pan?', 'What's next for Ireland?', 'Will the team party hard tonight?' Once it was over I sat down just in time to watch the highlights of the Zimbabwe game. While I had been involved in televised games before it was very strange watching myself on the replay, possibly because of the amount of camera time that I was given. It made an impression on me and from then on I was more cautious about my on-field behaviour. That night, JB and I had a couple of beers watching the highlights of our game again, as well as those of Sri Lanka v Bermuda. Poor Bermuda were given a lesson, losing by 243 runs. Mahela Jayawardene and Kumar Sangakkara had gone to town on their attack, while the Sri Lankan bowlers looked like they were playing against club cricketers. It wasn't a great advertisement for the so-called 'minnows'. It was also disappointing to hear the commentators criticising Dwayne 'Sluggo' Leverock. I have played against Bermuda on two occasions and although he's about twenty stone this guy can really bowl. I hoped that he would make those commentators eat their words later in the competition but it never happened.

The next morning started with a call to Vanessa and the kids. Vee told me that there had been great celebrations back at Ocho Rios the previous night. Mum was also in fine spirits, but the word on the street was that Dad may have been led astray by Matt Dwyer's little brother, Willie. After the call I headed down to breakfast. You couldn't keep the smiles off our faces and it was great to see the guys march one-by-one into the dining room. We looked at each other and laughed like schoolboys. I had a swim after breakfast and took it easy as our practice was to be a light one, as Adi and Matt only wanted a fielding session in the afternoon. I spent most of the morning flicking between England v New Zealand and South Africa v Netherlands. The Dutch fell victim to some record setting that day: Herschelle Gibbs hit 6 sixes in an over off Daan Van Bunge and Mark Boucher hit the fastest 50 in World Cup history. The Proteas ended up with 353-3 in a rain-reduced 40 over game. In the other fixture, Ed Joyce got a duck and England struggled to pass 200, never enough against a strong New Zealand team.

We boarded the team bus for Sabina Park and Big D was there at the steps with his hand outstretched. Even though our World Cup had only just kicked off you could tell the Jamaican public were warming to us and our style of cricket. They were waving at us and shouting: 'GO IRIE-LAND GO'. Peter Gillespie loved this and lapped up every moment, as did we all. I knew that I had damaged my shoulder when I had attempted to catch the second last ball against Zimbabwe. I had dived to my left and landed sharply on my armpit. I had semi-dislocated the same shoulder in the ICC Trophy in 2005 but hadn't had a problem with it until that moment. It was definitely sore, but for the time being I kept it to myself.

Adi and I had our usual press conference on the eve of a game. There were no particularly tough questions but there was growing interest in our performance. The world's media had by now featured Ireland on either front or back pages, sometimes both, and we were generally the leading televised sports story. It was great to see, but we knew we had only scratched the surface. I took part in training that day but only to hit a few balls. I iced the shoulder and got treatment from Knoxy, and by now we both knew we had an issue on our hands. Watching the boys field and catch during this session you would have thought the Aussies had put the shamrocks on for an hour or so. We just looked like a team that belonged in the World Cup, definitely not the 'minnows'. Adi was really pleased with what he saw and the training session was cut short. 'Well done boys, team meeting at 7.00', were his last words before we headed back to the hotel for a shower, food and more TV cricket.

Adi, Matt and I met at 6.30pm to discuss the team for the Pakistan game. With the wicket looking so green we discussed bringing in another seam bowler and leaving out Whitey. It would have been hard to drop a guy who had just got 28 runs and bowled the last over to get us home against Zimbabwe. Andy White and his room mate Kyle McCallan are very similar beasts, on and off the field, and for this reason they are known as the Spin Sisters. Andy is a bit of a practical joker, usually in tandem with Kyle. Their pranks are usually irritating things like nicking mobile phones and hiding shoes – the sort of stuff you don't need at the end of a game. We had our revenge in Namibia a couple of years ago when they came back to their room to find it completely bare – beds, bags, everything had been moved onto the balcony or into the bathroom. Peter 'Polish' Gillespie (his other nickname is Bubba the Love Sponge) filmed the guys doing it, although they wore pillow cases as hoods. The Spin Sisters reckoned it was Conor Armstrong and Paul Mooney and on the last morning retaliated in style. Somehow Kyle McCallan got a key of the Mooney/Armstrong room and kept it for three days, and finally sneaked up and took everything out of their bags, mixing their clothes and gear around.

Andy has batted from 1 to 10 in the order and would usually do a job for me with his gentle off-breaks. Whitey has become known as 'The

Finisher' as he was usually the man to bring us home in the big games. He moved to Northants to chase the dream as a professional cricketer and although he spent two years there, the combination of lack of opportunity and his love for playing for Ireland brought him home. He is as quiet as a church mouse off the field but sees the red mist when he crosses the white rope. Whitey is up for a battle against anyone and fears nobody.

We finally decided to go for the same team; unfortunately, John Boy had just missed out again. The team meeting went well, with input from Adi, Big Phil and Matt Dwyer. Matt gave his life to playing, developing and promoting Irish cricket. He made his debut for Ireland at the ripe old age of thirty-nine, and once he got the chance he proved why it should have come far earlier. He won 51 caps and took 62 wickets at a great economy rate of 3.8 per over, which are terrific stats for a spinner. When his international career ended he offered to help Adi as his assistant and made a huge contribution to the success we achieved. After we all had spoken it was left to Knoxy to remind the guys to manage their water intake in preparation and throughout the game. After the meeting I went to Knoxy's room for some more treatment and to stock my fridge full of fluids.

On the morning of the Pakistan game I entered the foyer to see a couple of familiar faces from my old club, Clontarf. Doctors Tom and Mary Coghlan were there with their son, Bill, and Roger McGreal and his son, Jack. They were pumped up after our performance against Zimbabwe and it was great to see some more supporters. Tom and Roger headed off to their hotel up the road to watch the last game of the Six Nations, which Ireland won only to see France steal the Championship with a last minute try. But my focus quickly switched from those guys to the big game. If we were ever going to beat the team ranked fourth in the world, then St Patrick's Day was always the day to do it. The bus trip was like a royal motorcade with the locals screaming and waving and Peter Gillespie again hung out the window soaking it up. Polish is one of my true friends in the Irish team and second only to Kyle in the list of Irish caps. His 47 ball hundred against the MCC in 2005 was the highlight of his career, but he has been awesome in games against the English counties in the last couple of seasons. He found it difficult to cement his spot in the Caribbean but continued to work hard on his game.

Before going out to warm up I dropped into the umpires' room to say 'Hi' to Brian Jerling and introduce myself to Billy Bowden, the umpire from New Zealand. Billy is a very funny guy and treated me just the same as he would Ricky Ponting or Rahul Dravid.

Knoxy always places four blue cones in a square in the middle of the field and we are told 'blue box, 8.25am'. We came together from our various warm-up activities at that time and Adi and I each said our usual bit about giving it our all, playing with passion, giving something back to the supporters and never giving up. The pitch was not a typical Caribbean one, as it was green and looked more like an English-style surface in late April. I knew if we were going to have any chance I had to win the toss. Roy knew this too, and at 8.45am he tapped me on the shoulder and said, 'it's time for you to win the toss mucker.'

At 9.00am I had my first encounter with Inzamam ul-Haq, a giant of the game with a record to match. Chris Broad, the match referee, spoke to us very briefly as did the broadcaster Rameez Raja, who would conduct the interviews at the toss. I tossed the coin and Inzi called 'tails', but heads it was. Without hesitation I said we would bowl. It was to be a crucial factor in the game. We could tell that Pakistan were not happy with the conditions as on a green seaming pitch the gap between the teams would inevitably close, especially with Ireland getting first use. When Bob Woolmer expressed his amazement at the state of the track I knew we had a real chance! Back in the dressing room I remembered I had to make a call to my Clontarf team mate, Bill Coghlan, to tell him where I'd left his tickets. Since the match-fixing scandal mobiles are not permitted and have to be switched off as soon as you got on the bus. The

ICC had an anti-corruption officer who would pop his head in now and again and walk through the dressing room to check we weren't on the phone or surfing the web. I had to talk to Bill, so I asked Roy to stand at that door to head off the ICC guy.

As DLS bowled the first over I positioned myself at mid-on. But four balls into the game I was in the doctor's room having my shoulder looked at. I had dived to stop a ball driven in my direction and landed on it again. The doctor on duty gave me a pain-killing injection in my backside. It certainly worked, as I could not feel my buttocks for twenty-four hours. But my shoulder was still in tatters.

From the start we were getting some terrible abuse from a group of Pakistani supporters, who suggested that we should stay in the pub. 'You guys are rubbish, just go and have a Guinness' was the mildest of their insults. DLS bowled a great ball that pitched on off stump and moved away from Hafeez, and Niall did the rest. Pakistan were now one down and, to our amusement, their obnoxious supporters promptly abandoned us and started on their own side. Younis Khan came and left when Andre took a great catch off a good ball from Big Boyd. The 6'8" giant from Bready is our fastest bowler and got near 140kph a few times in the World Cup. He first entered the scene a few seasons before but then disappeared to Middlesex, where he didn't make the breakthrough. After Boyd was released the former Irish coach, Mike Hendrick, invited him to Derbyshire and he was brought back into the Ireland squad towards the end of 2006. He took 2-23 against Italy in the European Championship and was then selected in the World Cup squad. During the training camp in South Africa, 'Stankin' really grew as a bowler, largely due to his intensive work with Hendo. His career really took off in the ICC Intercontinental game against UAE: in the second innings his pace and bounce even had me hopping at first slip and he finished with 4-56. He had a terrific World Cup, taking 12 wickets and causing real problems to some quality batsmen. His only problem is accuracy, but if he can reduce the extras and continue his progress he will have a huge future.

Then Nazir and Mohammed Yousuf put together a good partnership of 40, before I bowled a wide half volley and Porty did the rest at backward point. I was struggling with the shoulder but Mohammed had helped me out!

Pakistan lost four quick wickets for 16 in no time and we were well and truly in the game with the score reading 72 for six. Andre's spell was in the top three I have ever seen; 8 overs, 4 maidens, 5 runs, 2 wickets, it was in the Glenn McGrath or Shaun Pollock class. As we huddled for a drinks break, I reminded the team that, 'we were here against South Africa two weeks ago and we let them out of jail, we cannot let this happen today, we must stay focused'. Kamran Akmal came in and attempted to start a fightback. Akmal had scored four test hundreds and three in the one-day format, and I remember wishing he wouldn't do an 'Andrew Hall' on us. I also wondered where were those cricketing gods that Adi had promised us, because now would be a good time for them to show up.

Looking around the ground I soaked up the large emerald green patches in the stand – our fans, wild with excitement. I could even see the 6'5" leprechaun, Adrian Raftery, leading the conga in the Party Stand. It would have been easy to get caught up in the excitement, but we had to continue to focus. Akmal and Azhar Mahmood had started to build a steady partnership before Boyd and myself came together. Boyd ran in and struck Azhar on the shoulder, which really shook him up. I ran up to Boyd and told him to do it again. He did as I asked, Boyd ran in with his next delivery and bounced Azhar and he only hit as far as the 30m circle, straight up in the air to me at mid wicket. The dangerous Akmal was still there, but Boyd gave me more and dug another ball in short. Akmal took the bait and mistimed a hook shot, which I somehow managed to clutch running back and diving to my left. As fate would have it, I landed on my ailing shoulder. Kevin was first to reach me and I just lay there and told him, 'get Knoxy, get him out here'. I nearly ripped Iain's shirt off as he applied an ice pack to my shoulder. Pakistan were now 105 for eight but we knew that we had to finish this quickly because they had a top quality bowling attack. Kyle came on to bowl and removed Mohammad Sami before the substitute, John Boy, took the final wicket of Umar Gul off a skyer in front of the Party Stand. The fans went berserk and the Cayman Islands GAA fans were impressed when John soloed the ball back to the middle – Gaelic football style.

I remember walking off the ground, looking up at the scoreboard to see confirmation that we had just bowled Pakistan out for 132. I wondered if I was dreaming, but then I remembered seeing Bill Coghlan earlier that day – Bill would never feature in my dreams (he is a young twenty year old I played club cricket with for three years). If I had to criticise our performance that day it was that we gave away too many extras – Boyd had bowled 13 wides and altogether we had given Pakistan a total of 29 extra runs in a score of 132. It would have been a terrible injustice if we had lost the game by 2 or 3 runs.

Lunch came and went very quickly. I knew that 132 on that wicket could be enough for Pakistan, given the quality and experience of their bowling attack. Adi talked about the importance of getting off to a good start, as the ball would still be doing a little. He told the openers not to worry about the overs but simply to try to keep the scoreboard ticking over. Wickets in hand would be crucial. I turned to a group of players and asked them individually to consider the implications of not winning this game. I asked DLS and Andre did they want to return to delivering John Deere tractor parts the following week. I asked Kenny if he was ready to go back to sorting and delivering post, I even asked Kyle if he was ready to go back to the classroom, because I knew for sure that I wasn't ready to go back to selling fabric. For the first time I really felt that I had the squad's full attention: no one wanted this dream to end!

We got off to a bad start when JB was given out leg before wicket to a big in-swinger from Mohammad Sami, who then removed Eoin Morgan for 2 with a similar ball. We ourselves were now 15 for two, just as Pakistan had been a few hours previously. Eoin went into the World Cup with huge expectations placed on him by the media and the Irish fans. He had a disappointing time by his high standards but, like Jeremy, he got some good balls from some world-class operators. I believe Eoin Morgan is the best cricketer I have seen come out of Ireland. His concentration and temperament at the crease belie his youth and I am sure that he will play test cricket for England – and I would love to watch him do it, as long as its not against Australia. He is a real thinker about cricket and has the potential to score 5,000 Test runs. He works hard at his game and is always the last to leave the nets with his mate Porty. I enjoy playing cricket with this kid and I hope that we still have a few years left together on the field.

Happily, Porty and Niall O'Brien then put together a brilliant stand of almost fifty, denting the new ball and keeping the score moving. Porty was finally removed by the fifth bowler used, the off spinner Mohammad Hafeez. It was an unlucky dismissal as the ball was played onto the stumps. The fall of Porty's wicket brought Sami back into the attack, and saw probably the worst dismissal I have ever seen in any form of cricket. Andre Botha was given out caught at bat pad off Sami despite his bat being the width of the pad away from the ball. From the first ball the Pakistan team had appealed aggressively and exerted a great deal of pressure to get rid of Andre. Brian Jerling is a very good umpire, but the atmosphere out on the field that day was intense.

For the second time in this game the O'Brien brothers (Niall and Kevin) came together to set up our victory. The next 10 overs had it all – boundaries, sixes, unplayable balls, missed chances and rain, but the Railway boys stood firm. Niall probably played the innings of his career and truly broke the back of Pakistan. When I first saw Nobby back in 1995 I knew – and so did he – that he could be a very special cricketer if he could just stay out of trouble. The exposure to county cricket and four hard seasons in Sydney grade cricket, with two of my old clubs, made Niall into one hell of an all-round cricketer. A very tough and gritty batsman, Niall can also mix it with the best glovemen in the world. The two hundreds he scored were a big factor in our success in Namibia in 2005. If he can translate his energy off the field to his on field performance he will have another ten years at the top level.

The only shame about the Pakistan match was that Niall wasn't there at the end. We had been off for an extended rain delay and at that stage the Duckworth-Lewis rule would have seen us home. It was hard not to get excited as it was extremely dark and looked unlikely that we would take the field again. We did get back out, and the D/L calculations meant we had five runs less to get, but three overs fewer to get them. Niall raced past fifty and was on 72 after he hit the part-time off-spin of Shoaib Malik for six. But he tried to repeat the shot next ball, missed it and was stumped.

Andrew White and Kyle fell to successive balls from Iftikhar Anjum, which left us at 113 for seven, which meant we needed 20 runs and we had 12 overs in which to get them. While wickets fell around him Kevin O'Brien stood firm. This was an uncharacteristic role for Kev to play, as he is normally a run-a-ball batter. When I joined him at the crease he was as cool as a cucumber, and I knew if I could just stay with him we would bring this game home. The reduction in overs, due to rain, was significant as it also restricted the bowlers' allocation. Inzy had to take wickets and that meant using his front line bowlers. I turned to umpire Billy Bowden and said, 'this sure beats working for a living,' to which he replied, 'just don't throw it away, you've done so well.' Thankfully Kev saw off Sami's last 6 balls, and with Gul and Iftikhar already finished I knew we had it won. Even though they had the experienced Azhar Mahmood, Hafeez was bowling from the Pavilion End and wasn't troubling us at all. Azhar then came on from the Headley Stand end with six overs remaining and six needed to win. We just had to be patient. Even though DLS and Boyd can both hold a bat, it was up to Kev and me to finish off this job. Azhar bowled a slower delivery out of the back of his hand, which I picked up very early and swung through the ball. It hit the middle of the bat and disappeared over mid-wicket for six. I watched it hit the signage in front of the Party Stand and leapt high in the air. The only thing I recall after that was being attacked by Whitey, Eoin and Peter. All I really wanted to do was give Kev a hug and congratulate him on his performance, but I couldn't even get to him.

We were ecstatic and everyone was beaming. I had never imagined that we could enjoy a lap of honour more than the one we had completed two days earlier, but this was it. I ran over and hugged one of our selectors, Willie Wilson, and saw familiar faces from Belfast and the North West. Looking around the stands there were Malahide and Clontarf flags, our new friends from Digicel were there from all over the Caribbean, and most of all our family and friends. Adi came over to me and told me to hold out my hand, into which he slipped the match ball that I had just hit for six. Ian 'Gunner' Gould, the fourth official, had walked around the stadium to retrieve it and had handed it to Adi, saying, 'give this to TJ,' After the post-match presentation we turned to our supporters and shared a chorus of *Ireland's Call*. I try not to make the same mistake twice, so before the press conference, I tucked away a couple of beers for afterwards. The team weren't going to leave me dry a second time!

The press conference went really well and at this stage I was beginning to enjoy them. After the Zimbabwe match I had described the feeling as 'surreal', and on St Patrick's Day the same journalist asked me to describe this victory in a word. I told him that I hadn't done very well in English at school so I could struggle to find one for him. At this stage all I wanted to do was rejoin the lads and get on a bus to Ocho Rios. When I finally returned to the dressing rooms the celebrations were in full swing. They had to be cut short though as we had a long coach journey to join our friends and family. We packed our kit, dropped it back to the hotel and hit the road north. We picked up some refreshments at the Pegasus and with the songs flying the two-hour trip went quickly.

We arrived at the resort to a heroes' welcome. In the lobby of the hotel was a smiling wall of green. A few of us had decided to stay in our playing kit too, and although the smell wasn't great, no one seemed to mind. It took me just under an hour to make it from the bus to the check-in desk. With the press looking for interviews, supporters chasing autographs and families looking to congratulate us – it was an incredibly moving experience. I finally got to see my parents and cousin, Debbie, who were as excited as I was. Vanessa was upstairs trying to settle the kids, so I just dropped off my bag and joined the party.

The management at the Sunset Jamaica Grande had invited the squad to join their annual 'JamPatrick's Day' party, and we were delighted to do so. We were brought on stage, one by one, and introduced to a crowd of more than 400 supporters. Lanky did his Ferret Dance, which sent the crowd into hysterics. Roy took the microphone and thanked the resort and our family and friends for their support over the past three days and the last three months. He did a great job, as it would have been easy to forget someone with all the excitement of the day. Roy has given everything to Irish cricket and has at this stage occupied nearly every role possible: player, President, selector and team manager. He played 30 games for Ireland over a period of 18 years, which proves it's hard to keep a good man down. He gave a lot to the team and copped a fair bit of flak at times, but he still came back for more because he loves the game. It will be a sad day for Irish cricket when he hangs up his blazer.

When the formalities were over I got to spend some time with my parents. It was hard not to feel reflective about the journey that had taken me to Ireland and to this World Cup. There had been disappointments and risks along the way but that night in Jamaica it all felt worthwhile. I made a tactical decision to get Dad to do the drinks run as it was taking me on average half an hour just to reach the bar as everyone wanted to talk to me about the day. The support was fantastic but I really wanted to savour the moment with my family, and especially my Dad, who I hadn't seen for so long. A plot was underway to get James Fitzgerald – the former *Irish Times* cricket journalist and now ICC communications officer – into the pool. He was looking out of place in his ICC blazer, shirt and tie, which made him a sitting duck. In the pool he went, accreditation and all, although he just about had time to palm off his mobile, wallet and Blackberry. I suspected that I might be next, so decided to take the situation in hand and jumped in – having missed out on the post-game shower it was probably a wise move!

7 THE MURDER THAT WASN'T

The Jamaica Pegasus in New Kingston is a busy international hotel, rising seventeen storeys above the most salubrious area of the city. Other international hotels cluster nearby, hugging each other close for safety. The flags of the competing nations were hoist aloft in the lobby of the Pegasus, which was converted to a cricket theme for the fortnight that the city hosted the six World Cup group D matches. In the public areas, players, press and supporters relaxed in front of the several television screens that were permanently tuned to the cricket. But the prosperous and comfortable façade could not hide the fact that the violence of the city outside occasionally found its way inside its doors. Two years previously a twenty-three-year-old air steward, Wayne Brown, was found dead in his room with his hands and feet bound and ten stab wounds on his body. And the day after the CWC opening ceremony, a man described as 'a fantasist' secured entry to a black tie charity cricket auction in the hotel and ruined the evening with outlandish bids he was unable to pay for, before sprinting out of the hotel pursued by security guards.

Night falls fast and early in Jamaica, and it had just got dark when Bob Woolmer, the Pakistan coach, and his team pulled up outside the Pegasus in their lime-green bus. There were reports that the atmosphere on the coach was fractious, others report that there was stunned silence. Captain Inzamam ul-Haq said that, '(Woolmer) asked me on the bus when we were coming back to the hotel, "What are your future plans? Can we discuss them tomorrow?"' Bertram Carr, the driver of the bus, waited for a few seconds before letting the team off as a minibus taking Irish supporters and media to an out-of-town party drove away. It was 7.30pm.

* * *

Less than an hour earlier, as the formal press conference was wound up at Sabina Park, a BBC Radio Five Live reporter, Alison Mitchell, collared Woolmer as he left the room behind the media centre. The ever-obliging coach consented to one more interview.

Alison Mitchell (AM): What are your thoughts on losing to Ireland?

Bob Woolmer (BW): 'We batted abysmally, really – just made mistake after mistake after mistake. It just compounded, and eventually we were 40 to 50 runs short. That's sad because two-and-a-half or three years' work has gone in to this, and to fall out like this is very disappointing.'

AM: 'After the last World Cup, it prompted an inquest on behalf of the Pakistan Cricket Board and resulted in various changes of personnel. How do you view your future?'

BW: 'My contract runs out on 30 June anyway, so I'll sleep on my future. I have said that I'm reluctant to continue in international cricket, purely from a travelling [point of view] and so on, but I will stick to coaching at a different level. But I think a decision's probably been made for me.'

AM: "Made for you", in that you think you may be leaving before your contract runs out?'

BW: 'Well no, I'll talk to the PCB and [see] what they want me to do. If they want me to go, I'll go, if they want me to stay, I'll stay until 30 June. But I've got a contract, I'm not going to break my contract, but if the PCB want to get rid of me that's their business. As far as I'm concerned, I want to sleep on what I'll do, and what I want to do in the future in terms of cricket.'

'I don't think that just because I've lost this game, I'm any different as a cricket coach. There are a number of extenuating circumstances in the last six months as you well know, that have made coaching Pakistan slightly different to normal sides, so those are certainly things that I would have to consider. A lot of those things would have to change, a lot of those things, if I were to continue with Pakistan.

AM: 'If the PCB said that they'd like you to continue, would that make you more inclined to carry on?

BW: 'As I said, I would like to sleep on it a bit. We'll have a day off tomorrow and we'll just have a look and see what's happening. I try not to make too many decisions on disappointing days, you know, because they tend to be negative decisions. When you make negative decisions about your future, I don't think it's very good.

'I'll talk to the Pakistan Cricket Board chairman and see what he wants, but I think it's time, I'm nearly sixty now, or fifty-nine, and so I think it's time maybe to look at still coaching, because I have a lot of knowledge and I want to pass that on to people. Certainly from a coach [point of view], I don't think winning the World Cup is something I can achieve now, because by the time the next World Cup rolls round I'll be sixty-three and physically, you've got to keep going, you see, and it's difficult, it's not as easy ... '

AM: 'Won't quite be slippers and pipe at sixty-three, will it?'

BW: 'No, no, no, no, no, I want to continue coaching. I think it's time for me to start coaching coaches, start coaching people who want to play youngsters again. I enjoy that. I've been writing about the game recently, so I'd like to continue that, perhaps a bit of radio commentary or something like that available one day – who knows. As I said, I'd rather like to sleep on it, and it's a disappointing day for me.'

AM: 'It is rather, it sounds a little bit as if you've almost made up your mind without sleeping on it, that you have been pondering these things for a little while?'

BW: 'I have made up my mind, yes, but let me sleep on it first.'

*   *   *

After stepping off the bus, Bob Woolmer went straight to the Polo Lounge, just off the lobby, and had two bottles of the local beer, Red

Stripe. At 8.30pm he retired for the evening. It had been a long and stressful day since the team bus had left for the ground at 7.00am that morning. He had one final word for his captain, telling Inzamam, 'it is a sad thing we are parting this way.'

It is not known what Woolmer did in his room, or who visited him. He ate a meal, ordered from room service, may have drunk a bottle of champagne, and logged onto the Internet. He may have had difficulty sleeping, as he sent several emails throughout the night. At 3.12am he sent an email to his wife, Gill, at home in South Africa, who later said that he seemed fine, albeit upset about the loss to Ireland. The last email he sent was to his ghostwriter, Ivo Tennant, with whom he was collaborating on a revised edition of his 2000 autobiography, and articles for *The Times* newspaper in the UK:

> We might have to do this from afar. I don't know what is going to happen next. We will first play our game against Zimbabwe and then fly back to Pakistan. This will give me more time to work on my book on coaching. The articles will have to be more general from now on.
> Thanks
> Bob
> p.s. What a miserable day it has been. Almost as bad as Edgbaston, 1999!

Woolmer was coach when South Africa lost the 1999 World Cup semi-final to Australia off the last ball of the game, which took place at Edgbaston, Birmingham. Whatever happened in room 12-374 over the next few hours may never be known. What is certain is that Bob Woolmer's body was discovered by a chambermaid at 10.45am. A doctor and nurse attempted to revive him before he was rushed to the nearby University Hospital of the West Indies where he was declared dead at 12.14pm. The Pakistani media manager, Pervez 'PJ' Mir, called a press conference at the hotel and told reporters the news that the team coach was dead. He also shocked them by adding the details that Woolmer was found naked, and there was blood, vomit and faeces on his body, and elsewhere in the room. The Jamaican prime minister, Portia Simpson-Miller, came to commiserate with the team and left in tears.

*   *   *

As the news spread, tributes poured in from all over the cricketing world. His former team mates, and players he worked with, were generous and whole-hearted in their praise. Former West Indies captain and team manager, Clive Lloyd, said, 'the entire West Indies team is quite saddened at the passing of Bob, someone who we had high regard for as a coach, a cricketer and a human being.' Windies captain, Brian Lara, recalled his days working with Woolmer in English county cricket: 'I had a wonderful relationship with Bob at Warwickshire in 1994 and our relationship continued to grow over the years, even though we sat in different dressing rooms.' Ex-England spinner, Derek Underwood, said, 'He loved nothing more than talking morning, noon and night about the game and that is why he was one of the most sought-after coaches in the world. It was no surprise he went on to be the finest coach and manager in the world.' English umpire, Dickie Bird, said, 'Bob was respected worldwide. He developed into the finest cricket coach in the world. He knew the game inside out – that's what made him a magnificent cricket coach. I know for a fact that the Pakistan team thought the world of him.'

Ireland's Adrian Birrell had been an acolyte of the coaching guru from the days when he coached Eastern Province, while Woolmer coached South Africa. When Birrell was studying for his Level Four coaching badge in South Africa and England, he completed batting modules that were led by Woolmer. 'He was a teacher both on and off the field', he told *Belfast Telegraph* reporter Ian Callender. 'He had a life-long love affair with cricket. I never heard Bob speak about anything else but cricket. It was his life. He often talked about strategy, specifically about innovations. He loved this other way of doing things. He was a great innovative thinker. And little things, like bringing the sweep back into the game. While he was coach of South Africa, they went into all sorts of sweeps. I think the reverse sweep, though they were played before, along with the laps, the slog sweeps and all that is pretty much part of what he has brought into cricket. Everyone does it now, and I know people did it before Woolmer, but he used it as a strategy.'

Birrell told also of his last conversation with Woolmer in Sabina Park, 'Just after the game we had this memorable conversation. Bob was very gracious and gave huge credit to us. I told him we were lucky to win the toss, and he replied: 'Well, even if we had batted second we would have lost, because we batted so badly.' He said that we actually played better cricket. No excuses. I didn't notice anything untoward, he seemed fine. Obviously he was very upset, but fine otherwise. Just after the game against Pakistan, we went to Ocho Rios. I was spending the next day on the beach when I heard he had been taken to the hospital. Half-an-hour later they came to tell me that he was no more. It was shocking.'

*   *   *

Two nights before he died, Bob Woolmer was in good mood. A big, jolly character with one of those odd accents beaten into shape by a career that took him all round the world – he was born in India and educated in England – Woolmer was holding court in The Belisario Suite of the Pegasus Hotel. The occasion was a reception for the international media, hosted by the Pakistan team, on the eve of their game against Ireland.

Woolmer had not been having an easy ride from the Pakistani media, and his team was the most controversial in the game. Two star fast bowlers, Shoaib Akhtar and Mohammed Asif, failed drugs late in 2006 and both dropped out of the World Cup squad on the same day – shortly before the competition. Injury was cited as the reason but few believed that story. Their captain, Inzamam ul-Haq, had caused a test match to be abandoned in England the previous summer when he refused to accept an umpires' ruling that he had cheated by altering the condition of the ball. Woolmer had struggled to cope with Pakistani cricket. In most countries the coach played a dominant role, but it was Inzamam who ran the show – spiritually as well as in sport. Woolmer told friends he was frustrated that many players were obsessed by their religious devotions and that some would even leave the field to pray during a game. Most members of the Pakistan team had become devout Muslims after their ex-captain, Salim Malik, converted after his life ban for match-fixing. Inzamam and some others were members of Tablighi Jamaat, a Muslim revivalist movement, and listened to sermons on the bus to games. A sole Catholic player, Yousuf Youhana, also converted to Islam and changed his name to Mohammad Yousuf. Woolmer's dealings with Inzamam were complicated further because the coach spoke little Urdu and the captain little English. An irony was that Woolmer also found his previous relationship with a test captain – the corrupt South African Hansie Cronje (who admitted fixing internationals and was banned for life in 2000) – difficult to fathom. And religion also played a role there, as Cronje led many of his players in Christian prayer meetings.

In the Pegasus, it was disconcerting to see the room divided into brown and white factions. The Asian pressmen stuck to themselves, lined up along one wall, while Woolmer talked to the Irish and UK press at the other. It was reported that two Pakistani journalists had verbally abused him in the hotel bar, later that evening, for refusing to grant them an interview. Woolmer sucked on his bottle of beer and chatted entertainingly to the reporters. He gave a passable impression of an Irish accent in imitation of Emmet Riordan of the *Irish Independent*, and he was dared to do the impression at the post-match conference the following day. He laughed and suggested he might say, 'I tought tree-tree-tree for tree was a good enough score'.

He talked about the book he was working on, and the analysis he had done on the great players of the past. He chuckled as he explained how he had studied every one of Don Bradman's innings, all his writings and as much film as he could lay his hands on – and concluded that the Australian was so good simply because he never wanted to get out. Woolmer's work with computers revolutionised cricket coaching over the last decade, and he talked about this too. He mentioned his son, Russell, a designer who worked for Elverys, the Irish sportsgear chain. He also told the Irish reporters how he knew he was out of a job once this competition was over. His contract was up on 30 June, but he revealed that he had gone to his office in Karachi shortly before leaving for Jamaica to discover that it had been given to someone else.

That seemed so typical of cricket in that exciting but exasperating land. Dr Naseem Ashraf, the Pakistani Cricket Board's chairman, announced his resignation to the President of Pakistan and patron of the PCB, Musharraf, after the team were eliminated. Cricket is huge there, far bigger than any other sport; the route to vast millions for businessmen and enormous influence for politicians. It is also a rare way for the nation to show off on the world sporting stage. Arguably the greatest moment in Pakistan's history since independence was when the team, led by Imran Khan, beat England in the 1992 World Cup final. Imran launched a political career shortly afterwards although he was thwarted in his attempts to gain even a modicum of power.

*   *   *

Early speculation as to how Woolmer had died centred on the state of his health and the stresses he must have endured in his last days. He was a big, heavy man, with a florid complexion and type 2 diabetic condition, and had frequently complained of the heavy travel demands of international sport. After Pakistan left England in September they had played series in India, Pakistan and South Africa, before travelling on to Trinidad and Jamaica.

Former South African fast bowler, Allan Donald, was unconvinced that stress could have led to Woolmer's early death. He recalled how their coach coped with that traumatic defeat in the 1999 World Cup semi-final. As the players sat devastated in their dressing room, Woolmer went around the team one by one to remind them that it was only a game. Donald remembered: 'After that match we went back to the hotel and Bob tried to calm us all down. "We've only lost a game of cricket", he kept telling us. And he was right, of course. I watched his press conference after the Ireland match and it was exactly the same. Bob was obviously disappointed but he was also philosophical.'

The state pathologist, Ere Sheshiah, conducted the autopsy on Tuesday morning, and the results were announced as 'inconclusive'. The *Jamaican Observer* reported that a photograph of Woolmer's corpse showed marks on his right cheek, across his nose and on the left side of his forehead, just above his eye. Later that day, however, police revealed that new evidence had emerged that cast suspicion on the theory that Woolmer had died of natural causes. The Deputy Commissioner of Police, Mark Shields, told a press conference that there was new evidence that 'pushed' investigators to amend the earlier post-mortem. 'Having met with the pathologist, other medical personnel and investigators, there is now sufficient information to continue a full investigation into the circumstances surrounding the death of Mr Woolmer, which we are now treating as suspicious.'

On Tuesday evening, James Fitzgerald was interviewed for NewsTalk, the Irish radio station, by Jerry O'Sullivan. Fitzgerald, himself an Irishman, is Communications Officer with the International Cricket Council, based in Dubai. A former cricket writer with *The Irish Times* and *Irish Independent*, he had been delighted to discover that his first assignment at the World Cup would be in Jamaica, where his old colleagues and friends were based. O'Sullivan taped Fitzgerald talking about the death of Woolmer, and the coach's contribution to cricket in Ireland and all over the world. The pair were standing just outside the Polo Lounge in the lobby of the Pegasus. As they chatted, they became aware of a man remonstrating with them from several feet away.

Standing in the doorway of the lounge, he shouted, 'Tell him the truth, tell him the truth. You know he was murdered!' at a shocked Fitzgerald. It wouldn't be the last time the extraordinary PJ Mir would make his presence felt that week.

*   *   *

On Wednesday the Pakistan team returned to Sabina Park for their final game in the competition – a match that was at best an irrelevance, perhaps even a nuisance. Several players were reluctant to play, hoping that the ICC would cancel the fixture, but its president Malcolm Speed insisted the show would go on: 'What has happened is a challenge to the game to be resolute and strong and finish the World Cup in good spirit we will demonstrate that cricket cannot be put off by a cowardly act.' Several weeks later Inzamam ul-Haq complained, 'If this terrible tragedy had occurred in any other country, if such a security lapse had taken place anywhere else, they would have stopped the World Cup.'

While the result was irrelevant to Pakistan, Zimbabwe still entertained hopes of qualifying for the second phase if they won. Emotions were high at the almost empty stadium. The teams wore black armbands and stood for a minute's silence, with some of the players staring at the giant screen that showed a photograph of Woolmer. Others stood with heads bowed. The silence lasted well into the day, with supporters holding banners in tribute to the coach. One fan, Nadeem Khan, sat close to the team dressing room holding a green placard which read: 'Bob Woolmer lived and died for cricket. His true, honest, dedicated, devoted, sincere and hardworking services for the Pakistani cricket will always be remembered'. The supporter was told to put the sign away by stadium security, as he was told it 'was unnerving people'.

In the game the young opener, Imran Nazir, made a brilliant 160 but the biggest applause was reserved for Inzamam on his last appearance for Pakistan. The captain made a rapid 37 and was given a guard of honour as he left the field in tears. The total of 349 was far, far too many for Zimbabwe, and the Africans duly collapsed to 99 all out. 'We dedicate this game to Bob because he's a wonderful person,' said Inzamam. 'He's not in this world now and every Pakistani and every cricket lover is sad. I'm also very sad and that's why I'm emotional, also after playing sixteen or seventeen years. Thank you to my family and my father, who has supported me in good times and bad times. I will miss everything, the ground, the dressing room, everything.'

Back at the Pegasus, the Irish team spent the last hour of the game crowded around the TV sets in the lobby, relaxed and confident that nothing would go wrong at that stage and their progress to the Super Eights was assured. At the moment the Pakistanis secured victory, Birrell allowed himself a grin before the back slaps and handshakes started.

As the game in Sabina was unwinding, there were more dramatic scenes back at the team hotel. During a rain break in the second innings, the local TV station announced that one of its news journalists, Rohan Powell, had confirmed that Woolmer was murdered. Powell was in the Pegasus at the time and was immediately interrogated by his fellow reporters. A police statement followed that refused to confirm or deny the story, but said that they were seeking outside help before they came to a conclusive finding. 'Following consultations today, involving representatives from the Government of Jamaica and the police, a decision was taken to seek the opinion of a second pathologist', the statement read. The police had by then moved into the Alexander Bustamante Suite on the ground floor of the hotel, named after the first prime minister of independent Jamaica, a man who described himself as fifty per cent Irish, fifty per cent Jamaican and ten per cent Arawak Indian. Colin Pinnock was the chief investigating officer, but deputy superintendent, Mark Shields, an Englishman, was front and centre stage in all dealings with the media.

Later that evening a remarkable event was held in the ballroom of the Pegasus. PJ Mir told the assembled reporters beforehand that a private memorial service for their coach would be held, and that the players would not be answering any questions before or afterwards. He said the team had, 'gone through a lot of tension and mental torture' since the coach's death. The 'private' service involved the twenty-two members of the Pakistan party, who were seated to the side of the room, walking one by one to the podium to talk about Woolmer. Some of the players don't have perfect English, so Mir was obliged to translate. Two hundred journalists and broadcasters watched the private service in silence. Also present were some Irish players and officials, and Jamaican police officers.

Still wearing his playing gear, Inzamam ul-Haq spoke first, and was visibly emotional as he said: 'I miss him so much in my own life. He was a good man.' Assistant coach, Mushtaq Ahmed, described him as, 'a gentlemen and lovely friend'. Younis Khan, pinched his eyes and wiped away tears. Azhar Mahmood called Woolmer, 'passionate about his cricket'. Kamran Akmal's voice cracked and his eyes welled with tears as he told the reporters that: 'I'm going to miss him for the rest of my life.' Rana Naveed said, 'I pray that God finds him a place in heaven.' As each of the players made their way to the rostrum, the bizarre nature of the event started to become clear. The young men, most dressed in sweaters and jeans or casual sportswear, seemed genuinely shocked and upset at what had caused their grief and deeply uncomfortable at being forced to parade their private emotions in front of a worldwide audience of hundreds of millions. Why one of those leading the party felt the need for them to share those emotions in that way was never made clear. Some weeks later Inzamam criticised the Pakistan Cricket Board for not doing enough to support the players. 'The seven days we spent after Woolmer's death were the most tense of our lives. And we were surprised that the Pakistan board didn't rush someone out immediately to assist us,' he said.

Adrian Birrell, Ireland's coach, gave the fullest tribute during the ceremony. Birrell recalled the many happy hours he had spent discussing cricket with Woolmer and the enormous contribution he had made to the game. As Birrell returned to his seat, Inzamam stood up and shook his hand. When it was over, the players quickly filed out of the room, dodging the questions hurled at them by the media. Spinner, Danish Kaneria, paused to shake the hand of Irish assistant coach, Matt Dwyer, thanking him for his presence and wishing Ireland well in the second phase.

As the wildest rumours eddied around the hotel, news came from Ocho Rios of another tragedy. Bob Kerr, former president of the Irish Cricket Union, was found dead in bed at the Sunset Grande Hotel. In the atmosphere that pertained in Kingston, it became necessary for the Jamaican police to state that there was nothing suspicious about Kerr's death, and it was not linked in any way to the Woolmer killing. The death of the sixty-eight-year-old North Fermanagh official was a blow to the Irish team, most of whom knew him well from his time as the ICU president in 2004. Peter Gillespie spoke for the players when he said: 'There was no one that's done more for him from his home out in the west than Bob. Nobody has travelled more miles from Fermanagh, be it to Belfast, Ballymascanlon or Dublin, to sit in hours of meetings. He was just a true gentleman; a man of few words so when you did get a few words from him, you appreciated it.' Adrian Birrell echoed him, saying: 'This is tragic news, and on behalf of the entire squad and management, I'd like to pass on our sympathy and condolences to his wife Hope, and his family circle.'

*　　*　　*

At 6.30pm on Thursday (four and a half days after his body was found by the chambermaid) the Jamaican police finally announced that Woolmer had been murdered. The camped-out media were told to go to the ballroom of the hotel, where a podium had been erected. Mark Shields and Karl Angell were representing the Jamaican constabulary, Malcolm

Speed and tournament organiser, Chris Dehring, were representing the ICC. As the director of communications began to read a statement from the chief of police, the assembled press corps were each handed the two-page document.

As Angell read through the preliminaries of the statement, there were gasps as the reporters raced ahead to the third paragraph:

> The pathologist report is now available and states that Mr Woolmer's death was due to asphyxia as a result of manual strangulation. In these circumstances, the matter of Mr Robert Woolmer's death is now being treated by the Jamaica Police as a case of murder. Steps are being taken to conclude these investigations which include collecting statements from all persons who in the opinion of the police can be of assistance to these investigations.

The ex-Scotland Yard detective, Shields, told how person or persons unknown had gained access to Woolmer's room on the twelfth floor and killed him with such force that a bone was broken in his neck. Woolmer was a big man – 6'1" and over eighteen stone – and wouldn't have been easy to kill. The police said they were following several lines of enquiry, but were yet to detain a suspect. They also said they believe the coach knew his killer and that, 'those associated with or having access to Mr Woolmer may have vital information that would assist us with our enquiry.'

The announcement sparked off a storm of media coverage and wild speculation. The following day, a report in the *Times of India* quoted former Pakistani bowler, Sarfraz Nawaz, as blaming the gambling mafia on the Indian subcontinent for Woolmer's death. The ex-MP also named Pakistani players and officials, as well as ICC officials, as being 'deeply entrenched in match fixing'. PJ Mir was furious at his compatriot: 'Allegations are always baseless. Prove it,' he snapped at reporters who raised the issue. Birrell regarded as unbelievable the notion that Ireland's game against Pakistan might have been a target of match fixing. 'It has never crossed my mind,' he said. Trent Johnston, whose room was three doors from Woolmer's, was equally dumbfounded. 'It makes me feel sick to think about it,' he said.

Match fixing had convulsed the world of international cricket for much of the previous decade. Most of the corrupting has been blamed on bookmakers connected to crime syndicates in the mega cities of south Asia. Betting is only legal at racetracks in India, but bookmakers based in Mumbai are known to take bets on cricket totalling several billion dollars a year. In 2000 the Delhi police taped a conversation between the South African captain, Hansie Cronje and a bookmaker. The investigation that followed revealed that Cronje had accepted money to throw matches, for which he was later banned. Cronje later died in a plane crash.

The growing strength of the Asian economies, especially India, means the region is now the breadbasket of world cricket. Television rights for the World Cup brought in $2billion to the ICC, mostly from India. Such riches are in contrast to the modest sums paid to Asian players until relatively recently. Add to that a rapidly increased number of meaningless competitions – staged to satisfy television companies – and the temptation for players to play at a level short of their best is clear. Cricket has been in thrall to Asian gambling syndicates for many years. Millions of dollars change hands every time India or Pakistan play and it doesn't take much to subvert the result. The Cronje-gate scandal saw three of the nine captains of the test countries banned for life for taking bribes to fix matches. Players from well-paid sides, too, such as Australia and England, were also dragged into the scandal.

The ICC has a full-time anti-corruption unit and dressing rooms are tightly controlled during games. Players are not permitted to have mobile phones at matches and Internet access is forbidden. The change in the nature of betting makes cricket especially vulnerable, as gamblers have moved away from betting on a simple result and into the minutiae of sport. Cricket is a game with an enormous number of 'events' – each

One Day International lasts 600 balls and there are an infinite number of possible outcomes. A majority of soccer matches end 0-0, 1-0, 1-1 or 2-1, but there is no such probability in cricket. The twenty-first century phenomenon of 'spread betting' allows gamblers to bet on minor events in a match. It is easy for a corrupt player to influence these small matters which cost his team little. A player can put all his efforts into winning the game while fiddling on the side – and, crucially, a whole team does not need to be corrupted. For example, were the Ireland v Pakistan match to have been affected in such a way, it would not necessarily have concerned the result. The Pakistan team was on their way out if they lost and they bowled and fielded with such determination towards the end that it seems inconceivable they might have been got at. But that is not to say a bookmaker may have ensured a particular batsman was out for, say, less than 20 or a bowler delivered a wide in his first over.

*　　*　　*

The Irish captain admitted he had been losing sleep in an interview with *The Sydney Morning Herald*. 'It's sort of spooky. There wasn't too much sleep last night after the press conference where they escalated the investigation to the level they have. It's lock your door and that sort of stuff.' James Fitzgerald too, found his role dramatically altered as the cricket reporters became replaced by hard-bitten crime hacks. 'It's been a week of high stress and very little sleep', the former YMCA and Trinity all-rounder said. 'My phone just doesn't stop ringing, at all hours of day and night. Calls from Pakistan, India, Australia, all over the world. What I try to remember is that no matter how difficult it is for me, it is far, far worse for Bob Woolmer's family and friends.'

The Pakistan team were due to leave Kingston at lunchtime on Thursday for a short break in the west coast town of Montego Bay. The trip to the Ritz Carlton hotel was arranged before the tournament to avail of a short gap in the presumed schedule before Super Eights began.

Instead they were subjected to interviews, fingerprinting and DNA testing. The meetings took place in various rooms in the Pegasus hotel, and at least one took place at a shaded table beside the swimming pool. The team were eventually cleared to travel twenty-four hours later, with the team's fitness trainer, South African Murray Stevenson, staying behind. Robert Woolmer's widow, Gill, had asked him to look after her interests in Kingston. After a formal request from the Jamaican authorities, four officers from Scotland Yard travelled to Kingston to help, while Pakistan also sent a senior officer, Mir Zubair Mahmood, who had led the investigation into the murder by militants of US journalist Daniel Pearl.

The early doubts about the cause of death set the investigation off on the wrong foot. There was no sign of a violent struggle in the room and no visible bruising on Woolmer's body. 'If there had been any clear visible signs it would have been easier for us to determine cause of death,' said Shields. A Pakistan team source told *The Sun* newspaper that Woolmer was lying half wrapped in a towel, on his back, legs splayed and mouth open when he was found. It also reported that the hotel doctor said he was still breathing and initially believed he had suffered a stroke.

The original pathologist, Ere Sheshiah, was criticised by the president of the Jamaican Association of Clinical Pathologists. 'The final conclusion of this being a manual strangulation, I would not expect the first word to be inconclusive. Maybe they just didn't handle the thing properly,' said Dr Garfield Blake. 'Something like strangulation is clear-cut. Here is a gentleman of fair complexion. I would expect that great force would be employed to strangle, so there would be bruises, scratches on the neck or on the skin. That should be pretty clear cut.'

There was much speculation that the closed-circuit television images would identify a culprit, but these only covered the ends of the corridor on which Woolmer's room lay. The CCTV images were on VHS video, which needed to be converted to digital in case the original was damaged, and sent to the UK for further analysis. Woolmer's room remained cordoned off. The rooms around it remained occupied, but some guests were asked to move to other floors. Inzamam ul-Haq had been billeted there but had moved to the fifth floor 'to be closer to the players' shortly before the coach died.

The hotel's security was relaxed before the killing. There were porters at the main door and some men in the uniforms of private security, but there was little scrutiny of visitors. The night before the Ireland v Pakistan match a reporter visited Jeremy Bray, in his room, to confirm some details of his innings against Zimbabwe. Having been pass-keyed into the lift the reporter was able to proceed without any questions. After Woolmer's death armed police manned the entrances to the hotel and uniformed guards were stationed at each of the three lifts in the lobby. A guard travelled upwards with guests, who were asked to show a pass-key and were prevented from exiting at the twelfth floor. The resourceful RTÉ reporter, Robbie Irwin, keen to get a shot of Woolmer's doorway, simply got the lift to another floor with the guard and then took a second lift journey alone, down to the twelfth floor.

Several of the Irish party had rooms on the same floor. The rooms on that level are larger than those in the rest of the hotel, and were thus allocated to senior members of each squad and those requiring extra space, such as physiotherapists. Five of the Irish party were billeted there: Roy Torrens, Trent Johnston, Adrian Birrell, Matt Dwyer and Iain Knox – although all were absent that night. The Irish team had arrived back from the ground shortly before 8.00pm to leave their kit and make a quick change, and were on the winding road north by 8.10pm. They arrived back in the hotel at 10.00pm on Sunday. Police in Kingston interviewed Torrens briefly, while the whole party were asked, in Grenada, to give fingerprints and DNA for 'purposes of elimination' – more than a month after the killing.

Trying hard to be diplomatic, Johnston nonetheless expressed his team's relief at leaving Jamaica. 'The atmosphere in the hotel became very distracting,' he said. He met Inzamam for the last time, swopping shirts as he had done with all the other captains he faced. 'Johnston, the shirts are going for free,' Inzamam joked. Meanwhile, the Pakistan team packed up for a long journey home, although shortly before the party boarded the flight to London, three of them – manager Talat Ali, Mushtaq Ahmed, and Inzamam-ul-Haq – were questioned in Montego Bay after minor inconsistencies showed up in their initial statements.

Shields said he was powerless to keep them in Jamaica, and to do so, 'would have been to use a sledgehammer to crack a nut. It would probably have caused a significant diplomatic incident and had an extremely adverse effect on the World Cup.' Although he did insist that no member of the Pakistan team was under suspicion, he noted that he was in discussion with diplomats about what would happen should he want any individuals to return to Jamaica. He added that he would, 'cross that bridge when we come to it'. There is no extradition treaty between the two countries but in 1996 Pakistan returned a youth cricketer, Zeeshan Pervez, to Jamaica to face charges that he had raped an American woman in the Sutton Place Hotel in Kingston. The player was acquitted.

*   *   *

As the tournament moved away from Kingston – returning only for a semi-final in late April – the police investigation went on and eventually concluded that Woolmer had died of natural causes. The Pakistanis returned home to a derisive welcome and an unseemly game of pass-the-parcel as none of the senior players would accept the captaincy, which eventually passed to Shoaib Malik. There were services of thanksgiving for the life of Woolmer, who was posthumously awarded *the Sitara-e-Imtiaz* (Star of Excellence, one of the highest honours given to a civilian in Pakistan), by the government in recogniton of his contribution to sport.

In Ireland, Woolmer was remembered as a great and generous friend to Ireland, lobbying for extra opportunities for junior members of cricket's family. On the night he died, he told Trent Johnston that he was proud of the way Ireland played, although he was upset that it was against his team. Adrian Birrell recalled their last meeting at Sabina Park. 'He was very humble. His last words to me were that "the toss didn't matter. You would have won anyway."'

8 THE MORNING AFTER THE NIGHT BEFORE

At about 3.00am Vanessa suggested that we should call it a night. I was still in the cricket gear I had put on eighteen hours before, now wet from a dunk in the pool. I was shattered tired and moderately inebriated after a brilliant night at the Sunset Grande. We partied away St Patrick's Night with our families, friends and supporters, and in a blur as the achievement sank in. We were all brought onto the stage where Roy thanked all the supporters and Lanky gave them an exhibition of ferret dancing. As we wound our way to bed we had a long and slow stream of 'good nights' to share. We finally made it to our room where Mum was on the second shift, having relieved the Jamaican babysitter at around midnight. There were two double beds in the room with a child in each so I said to Vee, 'I'll get in with Claudia, you can share with Charlie.' My son kicks like a donkey and I wanted a good night's sleep. As I gently moved Claudia over and told her that it was me, she stirred in her sleep and whispered under her breath, 'I was so proud of you today Daddy.' Tears flowed down my face like a baby.

It was the morning after the night before and the kids were up extra early with the prospect of a day with Dad. It was 6.30am when Charlie screamed in my ear, 'let's go for a swim Dad.' There was no choice – I just had to get up. I turned on my mobile and I had forty-three text messages from friends and family around the world. It all came flooding back – we had beaten Pakistan in the World Cup.

Breakfast was the first stop of the day and we had barely left the lift when we were greeted by the restaurant staff. 'Where would you like to sit Mrs Johnston?' they asked. Vanessa whispered that this was unfamiliar attention. One by one the waiters, waitresses and management came over to our table to congratulate me on our performance against Pakistan. They had all been watching it and were as excited as if we were their own national side. I eventually got a breather to demolish a big greasy fry and prepare myself for a family day in the sun. By 9.00am the rest of the resort was beginning to wake and the media had appeared. I did an interview with Sky Sports on the beach building sandcastles with Charlie. It was all surreal but still fantastic.

What happened next turned the World Cup on its head. Iain Knox, Charlie and I were still on the beach front when Roy Torrens came to tell me that Bob Woolmer had been found unconscious in his hotel room and had been rushed to hospital. Forty-five minutes later Roy returned to inform us that Bob was dead. This quickly put our recent achievements into perspective. What we had achieved as a team and a cricketing nation was irrelevant, as a man who had been a driving force behind the involvement of emerging nations, such as ours, had just died. Bob Woolmer had been a forward thinker in the game of cricket and was a pioneer in many ways. He was a key supporter of the High Performance Programme and as such had paved the way for us to become involved in the international arena.

A few memories came into my mind that morning. I remember watching Bob throwing balls to Mohammed Yousuf in the lead up to a test last summer in England. He was bouncing the ball off a one metre square block of slate, to simulate the extra bounce they would face from the likes of Steve Harmison – a brilliant piece of improvisation. I also recalled what he had said to me after our victory, just a few hours before: 'You guys deserved that, I wish we could have won, but you guys played the better cricket.' This was a measure of a true gentlemen of the game. How could this day with my family, this tournament and our lives ever be the same again? Bob remained in our thoughts for the rest of our time in the Caribbean. The manner of his death and the protracted investigation that followed must have been horrendous for his wife and family.

While Claudia was old enough to understand that we had won, neither of the kids could understand the significance of the victory over Pakistan. They just wanted to play with me and slowly my mind moved away from cricket to give them my full attention, not knowing when our next day together would be. That day quickly came to an end and it was time to head back to see what was going on in the Pegasus. It was a two-hour journey back on the bus and the sound of silence was only broken by snores – the boys had well and truly 'tied the dogs loose'. We knew that we were returning to the scene of tragedy and we were all quietly contemplating what might have happened the previous night. The whisperings of suicide, murder, poisoning had already begun among the many media present and it suddenly felt a bit scary. We were all relieved that we had been so far away from the Pegasus on St Patrick's Night.

When we returned to the hotel I was swamped by camera crews and press from all parts of the globe looking for a different angle on the death. This intense media pressure did not end until we left Kingston some six days later. I escaped to my room away from the prying eyes and tried to get some rest. We had an early start the next morning, as we started our preparations to meet the West Indies the following Friday. It was only as I approached my room that I realised that Bob's room was three doors down the hall from mine. I had been aware that Clive Lloyd, Brian Lara, Danish Kaneria and all our management team were on the same level, but not that Bob was too. The heightened security was made evident by two officers with machine guns as well as two other plain clothes police officers. I had a very restless sleep that night.

At breakfast on Monday, I bumped into Pakistan players, Inzaman-Ul-Haq, Shahid Afridi, Azhar Mahmood and their assistant coach, Mushtaq Ahmed. I passed on my condolences on behalf of the Irish squad. After breakfast we were back to the grind with Adi, Matt and Simmo cracking the whip in an early session at Kensington Cricket Club. The couple of heavy blows I had taken to my left shoulder from diving catches and fielding stops during the Zimbabwe and Pakistani games meant I knew I was in a race against time to be fit for Friday. I really wanted to lead the guys out, as I knew the atmosphere would be electric and going head-to-head with the legendary Brian Lara would be a huge honour – and challenge – for me personally. I didn't want to miss out so my contribution to training was kept to a minimum, refereeing the touch rugby games and getting extensive physiotherapy from Iain 'Pretty Boy' Knox.

Knoxy joined us in 2005 and is always there for the players at any time of day and night. I remember a time in Kenya when I was struggling with a stomach bug. I thought I was getting better and asked Knoxy could I eat something, to which he replied, 'something plain and small.' So I got myself a ham and pineapple pizza. I had to call Knoxy at 3.30am to rescue me from the bathroom and had to promise him that I would listen to him in the future. Iain knows his stuff and is always looking to improve the way we prepare and rehabilitate. 'Pretty Boy' is a great guy to have around and is always quick with a joke or money-making scheme – making a fast buck is his one true passion. Watch out for him, he could become the physiotherapy version of Alan Sugar.

Deep down I knew there were major problems with my shoulder. I was not prepared to tell Adi or Knoxy (but I think he knew), that I knew I was out of this match against the hosts. Unfortunately, the Pakistan win turned out to be the last game my parents saw me play in the World Cup, and it was the same for Debbie, who had also flown half way around the world. That it was Charlie and Claudia's last game also hurt me big time. I was forced to put all that aside though, because I knew that I wasn't bigger than the team and that the team must always come first. At that stage we were still not guaranteed a spot in the next round. Zimbabwe could still beat the West Indies and there was already talk of Pakistan forfeiting their last game against Zimbabwe in light of recent events.

Monday night came and brought even more bad news about Bob Woolmer. The official attitude to his death had been escalated to 'suspicious', which essentially meant that it had become a murder case. I later attended the media conference with a couple of other players when the Jamaican police announced that it was 'Murder caused by manual strangulation'. The media circus went into overdrive – there was talk of mafia involvement, betting scandals and speculation that Bob was about to lift the lid on match fixing. I was even told by an Indian journalist that two Irish players had failed drug tests after the Pakistan game – which would have been hard as no one was tested. The only good news was that the West Indies had beaten Zimbabwe.

While I hadn't slept well on Sunday night, I slept with one eye open the next. I went up to my room, double-locked the door, put my cricket bags against it, and checked in every nook and cranny of the room. I even pulled out the trusted SS cricket bat and placed it beside me on the bed. The revelation that there had been a murder a few metres along the corridor was too much to take in. Could I be next? It felt as though we were in the middle of some bizarre Agatha Christie story.

We couldn't allow ourselves to get distracted by the unfolding events, although it was hard. We continued our preparation over the next two mornings, and again I did my best to get the Oldies over the line in the touch rugby with some biased refereeing. As it turned out we won the Jamaican leg, so the series overall stood at 1-1. My treatment continued over the next two days and while there was a small improvement it wasn't deemed significant enough for me to take the risk of further and more serious damage. Knoxy worked bloody hard on me that week, and I think he was terrified that he would have to tell Adi that I was out of the competition and should be sent home. We turned it into a joke at one stage, when we met Adi in the corridor. I whispered to Knoxy to tell Adi I was going home, and stormed off to my room without saying anything. Poor coach was devastated until we cracked up laughing.

A rare bit of good news was that the Pakistanis had decided to play the last game against Zimbabwe. After training on Wednesday morning we all went straight back to the hotel to watch Pakistan put on a display and a half. Thanks to Imran Nazir's 160 and Inzaman in his last ODI, Pakistan amassed 349. Zimbabwe got off to a bad start and were 14-3 before rain hit and their revised target became 193 off 20 overs. An old colleague of ours, Shahid Afridi, cleaned up the tail and Zimbabwe were dismissed for 99, a result that meant we had qualified for the Super Eights. That was obviously great news but it also put another twist on the Windies game, which became a de facto Super Eights game – the winner would bring the two points through to the next stage.

I went to see Dr Akshal Mansingh, the West Indian team doctor and a top orthopaedic surgeon, to get his opinion of my shoulder. He sent me to the University Hospital of the West Indies for a MRI scan, which was an experience in itself. I'm glad I'm not claustrophobic because it was a tight squeeze and spending forty minutes in the tiny cubicle wasn't pleasant. The scans revealed partial tears in the supraspinatus muscle. On the advice of the radiologist, an ultrasound examination was also done that ruled out a complete tear but revealed fluid in the subacromial space. Having discussed the advantages and disadvantages of a corticosteroid injection in this space with the doctor and Knoxy, we decided that this be done as the best way of reducing the fluid. I therefore had Depo Medrol and Lignocaine injected in the subacromial space, and advised to rest for five days before I tried bowling again. A Therapeutic Use Exemption form was filled out and sent to the ICC to make them aware an illegal substance was used as a last resort. Not a great finish to the day, but knowing that we were through made it easier to start planning my rehabilitation.

The day before the West Indies game some more tragic news filtered through from Ocho Rios: Bob Kerr, the former ICU president, had suffered a heart attack and died. He and his wife, Hope, had gone out of their way to make my first year in Ireland a very welcoming one and their warmth extended to Vanessa and the kids, which meant a lot. Bob always had a smile on his face and his knowledge of the game was outstanding. He unflaggingly travelled from his home in Fermanagh to attend ICU meetings and Irish games. I am glad that he was in Jamaica to see Ireland's first two games in a World Cup. Bob was a true gentleman and will be missed.

That morning we had a light session at Sabina Park. It was the first time I had bowled and it didn't feel too bad until about thirty minutes later, when I could not lift my shoulder at all. I was devastated and told Adi I was unavailable. Having qualified for the next stage my top priority was getting fit for those six games. There were mixed emotions at the team meeting on the eve of the game. My misfortune gave John Mooney his first opportunity, which was a massive thrill for him and his family and he thoroughly deserved his chance. John Boy is the sort of guy I'd have in the trenches with me everyday of the week. A gifted all-round cricketer, John Boy's stats don't do him justice and don't always reflect his contribution to the team. His One Day International debut was against England in Stormont when he collected the wickets of Trescothick, Bell and Collingwood, and followed it with 30 not out. He was very unlucky not to play more games in the World Cup, but he missed out on a couple of really close calls. In true Mooney fashion he picked himself back up and worked even harder on his game. Kyle also got the chance to lead his country out against the West Indies and go up against Brian Lara. Individually the guys came up to me to share the disappointment, which meant a lot.

I was dreading the morning of the game, and not just because I wasn't playing. I had an appointment to see the doctor on duty at the stadium, and I knew my phobia of needles would get a testing. Knoxy didn't help at all with his jokes at my expense. As it turned out I just needed two injections, so it could have been worse. On the field we got off to a great start with Kyle winning the toss and electing to bat. JB was the only batsman that looked comfortable against their attack. Everyone else got starts but didn't go on with it. We lost wickets at regular intervals before rain took seventy minutes off the second half of our innings. When it was fit to play we were left with only 16 balls to face and ended up with 183, which was never going to be enough. David Langford-Smith took the early wicket of Chris Gayle before Shiv Chanderpaul and Ramnaresh Sarwan put on a 120 run partnership. Kyle had Sarwan caught by Kevin at deep mid-wicket but some big hitting from Marlon Samuels finished us off. The atmosphere was tremendous with just under 12,000 people in the stadium, but our performance was not the send-off we wanted to give the Blarney Army. They had carried us through to the Super Eights with their amazing passion and support.

I knew David Moore, the West Indies assistant coach, from my early years in Wollongong, and he mentioned that Brian Lara would be happy to talk to some of our younger team members about his preparation and how he approached building an innings. Brian's visit was arranged for after the game when most of the West Indian team came into our dressing room to share a drink and a chat. Even their manager, the legendary Clive Lloyd, came along. It was a great experience, and not just for the younger members. To 'chew the fat' with two greats of the game was an amazing memory to take with us and we all really appreciated the gesture.

While we had lost this game, we had achieved a huge amount since arriving in Kingston. We were about to head to Guyana and enter the second phase but I didn't want the experience to end. I asked the players and support staff to gather in my room in thirty minutes, where I organised some beers and food out of the players' fund we had raised at a golf day in December. As per normal when free beers and food were promised, JB was first to arrive. We had a great night and plenty of stories were told. We were now ready for Guyana.

9 ONWARD AND UPWARD

In early January the Irish Cricket Union issued the players with a document that they would live their lives by from January to March. The programme told them everything they would do every day and where they would lay their heads every night. The last line read 'Saturday, 24 March', and was supposed to be the day they went home. But instead of heading for Montego Bay and the flight to London, it was off to Norman Manley Airport in Kingston to begin the long journey to Guyana and the first three games of the Super Eights.

It was a busy time for team manager, Roy Torrens. While the other seven international managers were busy organising press conferences and practice times, he was on the phone back to Ireland. 'I had to ring all the players' employers and confirm that they could give the players another month off,' he said. 'I wouldn't have liked to own a business that said "no". Given the euphoria in the country at the moment regarding the cricket team and the profile that the players are getting, I would have been very surprised if any had refused. We were fortunate that quite a few of the players' employers were actually out in Jamaica supporting the team and it wasn't a difficult question to ask. But you have to do these things and go through the proper channels. Kyle McCallan is a schoolteacher so we had to check with the education board that it was okay for him to stay out here,' Torrens said.

Former ICU president, Stan Mitchell, owns Dublin Grass Machinery and was happy for his delivery driver, David Langford-Smith, to stay on. Derek Plant's farm machinery company employs Andre Botha and Paul Mooney and he, too, was in Jamaica watching them play. Former Ireland captain, Angus Dunlop, employed Trent Johnston in his family's textile firm so he was more understanding than might have been expected when an employee rings up and asks for an extra five weeks off.

Other players had cleared the decks before the adventure began – Kenny Carroll gave up his job as a postman in October, although he remained employed by An Post. William Porterfield had taken a year out after graduating from Bradford University. Even the professional cricketers, Niall O'Brien, Eoin Morgan and Boyd Rankin, had to check with their counties that they could report back after the English season had started.

Rankin would normally spend the month of March helping with lambing on the family farm. 'My dad is just over the moon that we're in the Super Eights,' he said. 'I don't think he's too unhappy that I won't be coming home just yet. My brothers help him on the farm anyway. There's plenty of help so I think he's got things under control.'

*   *   *

Andre Botha walked up the steps of the Caribbean Airlines jet, his jaw dropping as the air hostess greeted him: 'Good morning Mr Botha, have you got your seat number?' Botha wouldn't expect to be recognised on his local bus from Skerries, let alone in Kingston airport. 'It's incredible,' he said to a passing journalist, 'they treat you like royalty here. In four weeks I'll be back in the Balrothery Inn and they'll be telling me I bowled shite.'

The ICC-chartered jet was packed solid with cricketing talent, dropping the West Indians off in Antigua and Sri Lankans in Trinidad, with the plane following the island chains down through the Leewards and Windwards. The various stops turned the flight into a seven and a half hour marathon, which ended in Georgetown Airport and a guard of honour by tournament volunteers.

The team were billeted in the Cara Lodge, a small boutique hotel close to the old Bourda Stadium. The players were surprised to be welcomed with a large banner with the tricolour printed on it, along with the slogan: 'Céad Míle Failte – Comhghairdeas agus go n-éirí leat' ('A hundred thousand welcomes – congratulations and good luck'). It transpired that the Cara Lodge was owned by Seán McGrath from Donegal and Dubliner Paul Cunningham, both of whom had been in Guyana for more than a decade and were married to local women. The homely welcome and comfortable rooms notwithstanding, the players were initially unhappy with the hotel. 'There was no swimming pool and no fitness room,' said Roy Torrens, 'which is a must for our players'.

An ICC official was summoned but it proved impossible to switch the booking. The problem arose because the hotel was selected by the Pakistani advance party, with the proximity of a mosque and *madrassa* in a strong Muslim district an important factor in their choice. All the other teams were based in the only two international hotels, the Meridien Pegasus and the newly-built Buddy's, both of which had the full facilities the Irish party demanded.

Happily, Seán McGrath organised for the Irish team to have full access to the pool and gym at the Pegasus and the party settled in for the seventeen-day stay, their longest period in one place – including home – in the whole time from leaving for South Africa on 7 January till their final return to Dublin 107 days later. It was a demanding spell, and not just because of three tough games against England, South Africa and New Zealand.

The Co-Operative Republic of Guyana is a poor country, the poorest in the region – its GDP is $4,700 a head (compared with Ireland's $43,600) and the comforts of home were not available for the players. Nightlife was limited to a couple of bars and three or four restaurants. There are no cinemas in Georgetown, although the lack of laws dealing with copyright meant that the latest Hollywood blockbusters were available on DVD for just over one euro. The Irish players were delighted to be there as qualifiers, and were just as happy at the warm welcome they received from the Guyanese, but after the lively fortnight in Kingston being surrounded by Irish fans it was difficult to adjust to a quiet suburban hotel.

Almost all the fans had gone home, their package trip ending after Jamaica. Many of the wives and girlfriends left too, although Ydele Steele (fiancée of Andrew White), Lynn McCallan, Ciara Gillespie, Joan Torrens and Maedbh Langford-Smith joined the players in South America. The media corps, too, was reduced to eight – 'We're a press puddle, too few to be a press pool', quipped Emmet Riordan of the *Irish Independent.* Just four supporters, Angus Hancock, Nick Roche and Douglas French-Mullen of the North Wicklow club, and Duncan Grehan of Knockharley, flew down to Guyana. They had an even more tortuous journey: the quartet spent four days in the Jamaican resort of Negril before abandoning a planned diving holiday to hop from Kingston to Barbados to Antigua to Trinidad to Guyana – a full West Indies test tour in two days, costing €2,500. The last leg proved savagely expensive as only first-class seats were available, but the four were not to be deterred. 'My wife Milla is Indian so she was very understanding, especially as we had beaten Pakistan!' said Angus Hancock. The four arrived in Georgetown on the morning of the England game, with ex-Merrion player Hancock disappointed to miss the early dismissal of his former team mate Ed Joyce. Hancock also played for Clontarf which ensured ex-team mate Andre Botha came across with the team's allocation of match tickets to help their harried budget.

*　　*　　*

The city of Georgetown is the most southerly of all the West Indian capitals, five degrees north of the equator. Although Guyana is on the

South American mainland, its status as the former British colony of British Guiana means it views itself as a Caribbean nation (as do its neighbours, French Guiana and Surinam). It is a member of the political union the Caribbean Community and Common Market (CARICOM), and plays international soccer in the Confederation of North, Central American and Caribbean Association Football (CONCACAF) region. The racial make up of its population marks it out as radically different from the rest of South America – about half the population is of Indian descent, with about thirty per cent Afro-Caribbean, a large population of mixed-race people, and a small Amerindian minority. There are significant racial tensions in the country, with several incidents flaring up during the World Cup. Like Kingston, there is a crime problem, with three times as many murders in 2006 as in Ireland, with a population one-fifth the size.

Birrell's men had a seven-day gap between the last game in Jamaica and their first in Guyana. The plan was to spend each morning training in the Bourda, the old test ground which had just been rendered obsolete by the new National Stadium still being built in the nearby suburb of Providence. Heavy rains, which seemed to arrive like clockwork at 9.00am, put paid to those plans on Monday and Tuesday, although some members of the party were delighted with the enforced stoppage on the second day. In the atmospheric wooden clubroom in the Bourda the players were approached by a tall, upright gentleman with grey hair. 'I'm Lance Gibbs,' he introduced himself – a name that sits in the record books as the greatest West Indian spin bowler and the holder of the test wickets record of 309 for more than a decade.

He asked to talk to the Irish spinners, and Kyle McCallan and Andrew White were delighted to be singled out. Matt Dwyer, himself a slow-left armer with 51 caps, also listened to the seventy-two-year-old Gibbs explain his technique. McCallan was fascinated by the encounter. 'It's always nice to meet one of the legends of the game, and interesting to see the state of his spinning finger. The way he grips the ball is completely alien to the way I grip it. He talked about gripping it hard, spinning it hard. I try to give it a rip but not the way he did. But it was a privilege to meet him, he still looks well and is a fit looking man.'

The Irish party returned the compliment on the eve of the England game when they went along to a ceremony at the Demerera club in Georgetown. The Guyanese prime minister and Mayor of Georgetown were present as an adjoining street was renamed Lance Gibbs Street. Although the England, South African and Sri Lanka teams were in town, only Ireland was represented at the event, and the mayor responded by awarding the freedom of the city to Roy Torrens, Matt Dwyer, Adrian Birrell and Barry Chambers the ICU's media manager.

There was trouble brewing in Providence when the Irish arrived in Georgetown. The local Sunday newspaper, *Kaiteur News*, and a BBC website speculated that the ICC had made plans to switch the six Super Eights games away from Guyana. The chairman of the Local Organising Committee was sidelined, but the spanking stadium and adjoining international hotel were in varying degrees of completion – less than twenty-four hours before the first game in the stadium. Sri Lanka v South Africa was due to take place on the Wednesday, but a visit to the ground, the day before, found a furious English official attempting to find workers who had arrived to install Internet access and telephone lines. Huge areas of the surrounds were criss-crossed with trenches and pot holes, but inside the stands all seemed ready for the big event.

RTÉ television reporter, Robbie Irwin, filmed the final preparations, and dodged the ICC officials to record an interview with umpire, Steve Bucknor, on the edge of the square. The veteran Jamaican had umpired the four previous World Cup finals – and would stand again in a fifth – and expressed his delight at Ireland qualifying for the second phase. 'They play great cricket', he told RTÉ. He also remembered that he had learned a song in school called, *When Irish Eyes Are Smiling* and proceeded, quite surreally, to wander off singing it with a jig in his step.

Back at the Cara Lodge, more trouble was in the air as an innocent photograph threatened to become an international incident. Eoin Morgan stopped to chat to the armed guards at the hotel entrance, and one handed him his M16 machine-gun. Barry Chambers was passing and snapped the policeman and Morgan posing with the gun. Chambers had been supplying photographs from Guyana to the Dublin picture agency, Inpho, and the photo of Morgan was among several sent that day of players training and relaxing. The following day the photo appeared in several Irish newspapers, most prominently in the *Irish Examiner*. Somehow the word of this got back to Guyana and a furore erupted in the local media. The state television station reported that night that the policeman had been sacked, which horrified the Irish party.

'I was sick,' recalled Chambers, 'that a man, a father of children, could lose his livelihood over something like this was very distressing. I can honestly say that I felt as bad as I've ever felt in my life.' With Roy Torrens and Adrian Birrell, the media manager requested a meeting with the chief of police, Hamilton Greene, to plead the case of the guard. 'Adrian was fantastic,' said Chambers, as the senior policeman explained that the guard had been censured but would not lose his job.

Morgan wrote about the incident in his CricketEurope blog: 'I have learned a lesson and you will not see me with any more M16s this tournament. Instead it will be DVDs and, er … more DVDs. Given that we are not really allowed out of the hotel, there is not exactly a lot to do here. In fact they might as well have put us in the Sahara. So the TV it is. So far I have been through two series of 'Two and a Half Men', nearly completed four series of 'Scrubs', just started a new series of 'Life As We Know It' and probably six series of 'Friends'.'

Three days later, at the Ireland v England game, a security guard stopped a spectator who was carrying a bottle of water. The fan wasn't happy at the officiousness and told the guard: 'You let Morgan have a machine gun man, and you won't let me bring in a bottle of water!'

The team were delighted to hear about how the Irish public were reacting to the new success of the cricketers and were even more pleased when the team sponsor, Bank of Ireland, announced they would put another €50,000 into the players' pool. Tom Hayes, chief executive of Bank of Ireland Corporate Banking, said: 'Over the past two weeks the game of cricket has been embraced by all sports lovers on the island of Ireland. We extend our sincere congratulations to Adrian Birrell, Trent Johnston and all the team on its progression into the top flight of world cricket and we look forward to the matches ahead.'

There was another nice bonus on the way too. The Digicel mobile phone firm, owned by Dubliner Denis O'Brien, are $18.75m sponsors of the West Indies team, but were not allowed proclaim this during the World Cup because they were in competition with an ICC sponsor, Cable & Wireless. The team were visited in their hotel by Liam McDermott, Digicel's Director of Business Development and a former rugby player with Wanderers, who told them that Denis O'Brien would make a £5,000 (€7,500) gift to each member of the playing and coaching team in recognition of their efforts. The company played another role in Guyana, with their Irish employees boosting the tiny group of supporters in the Party Stand. Mia Fitzgerald from Bagenalstown, County Carlow, enjoyed her first experience of the sport: 'We were all dressed in green for the games and had a great time in the Party Stand. It was great to be Irish and we got all the Guyanese on our side too.'

Another visitor to the Cara Lodge was Prince Andrew, on a private visit to Guyana. After lunching in the hotel restaurant, he stopped to chat to Roy Torrens and Barry Chambers, and told them he had been following Ireland's progress on television. 'You have enhanced the cup with your spirit, and it's great to see a team with a smile on their faces.' They chatted about cricket and rugby, with the prince interested in the fact that cricket is organised on an All-Ireland basis. As he left, Torrens headed for the restaurant – 'I'll have to see what he ordered. If it's good enough for the Royal family, then it's good enough for me!'

Over on the other side of Georgetown another Irishman was getting ready to play cricket *against* the land of his birth. Ed Joyce's career had taken some huge steps forward after helping Ireland qualify in the 2005 ICC Trophy. The following winter he had been selected for the England 'A' tour of West Indies and in 2006 he made his full One Day International debut, coincidentally against Ireland at Stormont. A nasty ankle injury held up his progress but he was called up for the Ashes series in Australia when Marcus Trescothick pulled out in the first week of the tour. Joyce didn't play in that disastrous 5-0 defeat, but was a key figure in England's revival in the one day series that followed. England had lost five of their first six games when they came to Sydney. Joyce was on 6 when he hit the ball in the air to Shaun Tait standing on the boundary, but the Australian inexplicably dropped a straightforward catch. Seizing his second chance, Joyce went on to make a match-winning 107. 'My hundreds with Ireland do not compare to this,' he said after the game. 'It was an amazing feeling doing it here in Sydney against Australia. It is probably the best feeling you will get in cricket. My innings against New Zealand the other day helped relax me and I had a bit of luck early on. One hundred does not make a career but hopefully there will be more in the future.' England stunned Australia by winning the Commonwealth Bank series, and Joyce won a place on their World Cup squad.

His competition started with 1 against New Zealand before he top-scored twice, 66 against Canada and 75 against Kenya, but his place was still under threat. The English media was unhappy with the poor cricket their side was playing, and had identified a lack of aggressive batting from the top three as the main problem. Joyce was outscoring the other two, Ian Bell and Michael Vaughan, but was still the most vulnerable. Vaughan, as captain, was undroppable, and it was his repeated failure to score runs that eventually cost Joyce his place.

The Dubliner – his family moved to Bray, County Wicklow, when he was a toddler – was wheeled out two days before the Ireland game to face a barrage of media questions. First he was filmed for television in the hotel garden, then probed by radio in the dining area. Finally he was led by the England and Wales Cricket Board (ECB) media manager, Andrew Walpole, to a conference room where he faced the print journalists. He handled the conference well, having the answers on his changed allegiance polished from years of practice. He admitted that his England debut at Stormont was 'difficult, and emotionally quite strange', and said he expected to feel 'odd playing against my countrymen'. He pointed out that he got a bit of stick in Ireland, but only from people that don't understand the way cricket is organised and why he made his decision. Joyce has ambitions to play Test match cricket, the ultimate form of the game and one he would never have been able to reach had he stayed with Ireland. He also explained that he had talked to the England coaches about his former team mates, which drew a witty riposte the following day at an Ireland press conference. Kyle McCallan announced that he had been, 'out for a beer with Joycey and he's told us all the England plans.' There was a moment's silence before McCallan unveiled an enormous grin.

Back home, the Irish media were latching on to the Joyce angle with gusto. His parents, brothers and sisters were widely quoted on their divided loyalties, but his father, Jimmy, played straight with his comment that 'the perfect scenario would be for Ed to score a lot of runs but for Ireland to win'. Ed's mother, Maureen, was just as conflicted: 'I have very mixed feelings about it all, but mostly I want Ed to succeed. It caused a pang when Ed declared for England, I admit, but Ireland's success has been fantastic and its doing great things for the sport here.'

The impending game with England also brought the Irish players into the sights of the UK media, and their attentions were at times more than an irritation. While the players were generally happy to answer media requests, the increasing number got out of hand. Most nights Bray and Johnston found their sleep interrupted by Australian radio stations keen to mull over the novelty of the New South Wales Irishmen. The Irish captain was less keen to discuss his changed loyalties with the UK press, who were at times sneering about Ireland's achievements.

The early patronising talk of 'minnows' from Sky Sports Commentator, Michael Atherton, and Michael Holding was replaced by taunts of 'mercenaries' by a third commentator, Paul Allott. Johnston was furious, but was persuaded to avoid confrontation ahead of the game. Vice-captain, Kyle McCallan, came to the next press conference, and gave a passionate and reasoned read on the criticism:

> These guys are not mercenaries who have flown in for the World Cup. They have contributed to Irish cricket over a prolonged period and hopefully whose kids in time will contribute to Irish cricket. Trent is married to an Irish girl with two Irish kids; Jeremy Bray has lived in Ireland as long as I can remember, as has Andre Botha.
>
> People are entitled to their opinions but in a small way it motivates us even more. Particularly the guys that are born and bred in Ireland, they want to show that they can compete at this level and I feel they have done and will continue to do so. We beat Pakistan fairly and squarely. Niall O'Brien scored 72 not out and Boyd Rankin got 3-30 — two born and bred Irishmen.

McCallan drew a parallel between Johnston and England's South African-born batsman Kevin Pietersen. 'We miss Trent Johnston when he doesn't play but I imagine England would miss Kevin Pietersen if he doesn't play for them and there's no difference whatsoever.' he said.

Johnston reserved his comments for those who said Ireland didn't deserve a place in the last eight. 'It has added fuel to the fire. We were told we didn't deserve to be in the competition when it first started. Now they're saying we don't deserve to be in the Super Eights,' he said. 'We had to win two games, or tie one and win one, to get through and we did that. We're living a dream and the experience we'll take from these next six games is going to be huge for the guys and for Irish cricket.'

Ireland v England games at all sports are fought with the tensions of local derbys, with the added frisson of history and politics. At times they have exploded into violence, but the rugby game between the teams, a few weeks earlier, was a joyous celebration. With no more than a dozen Irish fans, this was never going to be a replay of the Croke Park game.

10 ALL ABOARD THE GUYANA EXPRESS

Saturday, 24 March 2007 was the day all our lives changed, the day we flew to Guyana for the Super Eights. We had proved nothing is impossible in sport. In Georgetown we were booked into the Cara Lodge Hotel, which we were surprised and delighted to see was run by an Irishman, Seán McGrath. We noticed immediately that we no longer had the strong support base that we had in Jamaica, and the first few days were a bit downbeat as most of us had to say goodbye to our families, who had returned to Ireland. Dave Langford-Smith's wife, Maedbh, had a nightmare trying to rejoin us, as she had to fly via Miami and several West Indian islands. Dave was quite upset by the hassle and delighted when she finally arrived at the Cara Lodge.

The weather wasn't good for our first few days in Georgetown, but we managed a bit of practice between the showers. We got a bit of outdoor work done but it was an indoor session for a hour and that was cut short as we had double booked the facility with Sri Lanka, and with them being the senior team and a game the next day we left without a fuss. Phil Simmons's local knowledge and contacts were more than useful one afternoon when he took us along to King's Jewellers for a bit of shopping. This is a regular destination for visiting cricketers and there was some serious bling on display. I think Vanessa was delighted with what she got!

My dodgy shoulder continued to give problems, but two days before the first Super Eights game I was able to complete a three-hour training session without any pain. I bowled five overs and that made me confident that I would be alright on the night. Dave had been having back spasms so he took it easy at nets, bowling off a shorter run. After training we visited the brand new Providence Stadium, the centre of our universe for the next three games. The stadium looked unfinished from the outside but is beautiful within – and what an atmosphere. We watched South Africa seemingly cruise to victory over Sri Lanka, before Lasith Malinga took four wickets in four balls. The South Africans squeaked a win by one wicket, but a couple of our guys missed the breathtaking finish. Jeremy Bray has the attention span of a gnat and kept complaining he was bored as the game drew to a close. He got so restless that he headed off and missed the best finish of any game in the competition – except for a couple that we were involved in, of course.

The day before the game I had my first encounter with the UK media; and I had a fair idea what they wanted to talk about: (1) the Irish players who weren't born in Ireland, (2) the English player who was, and (3) what right did we have to be in the Super Eights anyway? I don't really read the papers when I'm away on tour but I'm kept informed by Barry Chambers, our media manager, and a bloody good one at that. We knew we had plenty of begrudgers such as Mike Atherton and Michael Holding of Sky Sports and Jonathan Agnew of the BBC, who seemed to resent us being there. To be honest, we didn't care anymore at that stage; stuff like that motivated us even more and made me even prouder of the team. Normally I went to the press conferences with Adi, but on that occasion Kyle wanted to go along. He felt very strongly about the non-Irish born players question and let the begrudgers have it with both barrels.

Kyle 'Queenie' McCallan is a magnificent guy to have as a deputy. He is known as Mr Dependable, as he has only missed two games for Ireland in the last ten years, and neither of them were due to injury. His consistency, durability and passion is one of the reasons why Ireland are the team they are today. Kyle led the team for two days in Namibia, after I broke my finger, and his leadership helped us to win that trophy. He very rarely goes for more than four runs an over, no matter who the opposition is. Kyle had a good World Cup and ended up with 10 wickets at 23. A very capable batsman too, he has batted from 1 to 10 during his career and has already passed the 3,000 run mark for Ireland. Unfortunately, his batting wasn't at its best during the World Cup and he managed to equal AB de Villiers's record for the most ducks in the tournament with four. I can't imagine an Ireland team playing without the name McCallan in it for years to come. It will take some cricketer to fill his boots. It's a mystery to me how Queenie didn't secure a county contract five years ago. He would even be a great proposition now.

Dealing with the off-field stuff was tough at times. I was on call virtually 24/7 as most nights I got a phone call from an Australian newspaper or radio station looking for an interview. It was great that Australia adopted us as their second team, but sometimes when the phone rang I thought of letting it go. But I knew it was important – we were out there promoting Irish cricket. It was an once-in-a-lifetime opportunity to tell the world about us. I couldn't let it go.

My shoulder held up and I came back into the team for John Boy, but my luck ended when the Sri Lankan legend, Ranjan Madugalle, tossed the coin and it came down again on the side that Michael Vaughan had called. I lost six out of eight coin-flips at the World Cup, but then I was always a useless tosser.

England decided to bat first and we got off to a cracker of a start when big Boyd Rankin bowled Ed Joyce, who wasn't playing a shot, and then removed skipper, Michael Vaughan, the very next over. In strolled Kevin Pietersen and he and Ian Bell consolidated England's position before they were dismissed with the total on 119 for four. At that stage I thought we could get them out for under 200, but England's two quality all-rounders, Paul Collingwood and Andrew Flintoff, put on around 80 for the fifth wicket. I eventually got to perform the – now-legendary – chicken dance for the delighted locals after I bowled Freddie Flintoff. If only we could have stopped the game there!

The last 10 overs were a nightmare. We conceded 94 runs, which was way too many, and suddenly England were virtually out of sight. The cruel thing about this sport is that it is only a matter of millimetres between success and failure: a millimetre too short or a millimetre too full and you're punished. Against a guy like Paul Collingwood you have to be spot on and unfortunately we weren't. It's up there on the scoreboard for all to see: 94 runs off 10 overs. Ouch! The night before the game the rest of the guys were talking about Pietersen, Flintoff and Joyce – but I had spoken about Collingwood as the danger man. He always does something, whether with bat or ball or in the field. But talking about dealing with him and doing something about it are entirely different things and on the day we just couldn't cope with his class. Collingwood got 90, and Nixon and Bopara chipped in at the end, too. They set us a target of 266, about thirty more than we reckon we could have chased.

Our innings got off to the worst possible start with Jeremy Bray and Eoin Morgan back in the hutch with the score on 11. Will Porterfield and Niall O'Brien got back on track with a partnership of 61, before Flintoff ended their good work. We had steady partnerships along the way but kept losing wickets at critical times. Andy and I were feeling comfortable and put on 60 runs, with some big hitting off James Anderson and Sajid Mahmood. But Vaughan brought back big Fred and he rearranged my wicket. I think that was a sign that we had them in trouble, that Vaughan realised he had to go back to his A-team. Suddenly we were facing 140km/h in-swinging yorkers. You don't get many of those at Park Avenue playing for Railway Union against Merrion! As I walked back to the pavilion Flintoff tapped me on the back and said, 'Well played big lad.' Andy White kept going but the end was nigh and we were bowled out for 218, with Flintoff taking 4-43.

We knew where it went wrong: our bowling at the death just wasn't good enough and our batsmen got bogged down against Flintoff and their spinners. All the commentators said that our top order batsman would struggle against the pace bowlers in the Caribbean, but it was spin bowling that squeezed us. We just are not used to spinners of that class, especially on the kind of almost Asian-style wickets we came up against there. If we had only scored runs off the spinners we could have done something really special that day. That's a big if, of course, and an even bigger learning curve. After the game I told the press that I hoped fewer people were questioning our right to be there. Certainly Michael Vaughan wasn't questioning it. He knew he'd been in a game.

The morning after I was beaten but not bowed. My body ached and my head felt dusty from last night's beers. But I didn't feel down, especially when I checked the papers that were shoved underneath my bedroom door. The headlines were kind: 'Ireland make England work for 48-run victory', 'Vaughan gives Ireland credit', 'Collingwood and Flintoff spur England to victory'. But the headlines didn't tell of our disappointment. Little things jumped into my head – we had England 20 for two and then 110 for four. We *had* them. It would be Pakistan all over again. Then along came Collingwood and Flintoff and the end of my dream. A player as brilliant as Andrew Flintoff came in at No 6 – how ridiculous is that? Still, we had them worried. From where I was standing they seemed nervous. I was disappointed, but happy and proud of the team. We didn't beat England, we didn't do another Pakistan – but it was another good day for Irish cricket.

We went to the Pegasus Meridien for a long recovery soak in the pool. Adi made it a voluntary session, but nearly everybody turned up. I saw little things that filled me with hope – the batsmen all wanted to discuss ways of dealing with spinners. Andre wanted to sit down and have a word about how we can improve our bowling. Andre is a very similar cricketer to Kyle. A miser with the ball, he's my 'go to' man in the final stages of a one-day game. He has such control – it's sometimes as if the ball is on a string. A famous comment he made, which will stay with me for as long as I'm around, was when Dwayne Bravo hit him for six at Stormont. The shot enabled the West Indian to bring up his hundred off the last ball of the innings, after which Andre turned to me and said, 'Does anybody else bowl in this team?' Andre 'Chisel Chest' Botha is a huge scorer of runs in domestic and international cricket and his 157 played a big part in the victory over the UAE in Dubai, just before the World Cup. Andre had a good World Cup until he strained his hamstring in a warm-up to a practice session, which put him out for three games. He is the only man I know who has threatened retirement more than fifty times while actually out on the pitch. Andre is 'Old School'; nothing too flash but he gets the job done year after year, game after game.

The micro-climates of Georgetown played a weird trick on us on Sunday. Our training session at Everest CC was abandoned after forty-five minutes due to torrential rain – just as West Indies and Sri Lanka played in Providence without interruption. The grounds are about 5km apart. There were other tricks in the air too, especially as it was April Fool's Day. Kyle McCallan and Andrew White are the comedians of our party, forever coming up with practical jokes, but that day they were on the other end of the gag. They received word that Christopher Martin-Jenkins, the doyen of English cricket writers, wanted to meet them at the Windies Bar and Grill for an interview at 2.00pm. This was such a kick for them that they got dressed up in jeans and collared shirts and headed off to the Windies Bar and Grill to wait. And wait. They continued to wait but he still hadn't appeared. Then at 2.30pm they got a message saying Martin-Jenkins was running late and they were to order whatever they liked from the bar. Half an hour later we took them out of their misery with a barrage of text messages: 'APRIL FOOLS!' They warned us that retribution would be swift and brutal. But we didn't mind, we were one up.

The eve of the South African game gave me a rare day-off from the media commitments. The pressmen requested that Adi and Andre Botha come to the conference and that was fine by me. The touch rugby was won by the Youngies in controversial circumstances but we still held the upper hand in the series. JB, Lanky, Maedbh, Matt and I went to the Pegasus Hotel to use their swimming pool and got talking to the South African bowler, Andre Nel. He told us about his disappointment on not being in the team despite performing well. He couldn't work it out. He didn't dwell on it, though, and kept training hard, waiting for his chance. If he gets it he'll take it with both hands. That's what a real team man is: one who takes the good with the bad and gets on with it. We had our normal team meeting later and were blessed to have plenty of good intelligence as Adi and Andre know their players inside out. We finished the meeting with a replay of the highlights of the tour up to then, which brought plenty of smiles to the guys' faces.

Paul Mooney came in for his first game in the World Cup, at the expense of Kevin O'Brien, which meant we all slid up one place in the batting order. We were very keen to bowl first, but yet again I lost the toss and we were asked to bat. Again we got off to a bad start as JB got another duck. The South African attack of Shaun Pollock and Makhaya Ntini are a handful on any wicket, let alone one as lively as that, so it was a huge achievement for William 'Porty' Porterfield and Eoin to survive the next 11 overs, before the first of several rain breaks came with the score on 23 for one. Rain is a constant pain for cricketers, and there are complex rules (the dreaded Duckworth-Lewis calculations) that come into operation when it arrives. When the ground became playable again we were told we had just 24 more overs to bat, which meant we were really up against it to post a good score. It is always hard to come back out to bat after a rain break, as the bowlers have had their feet up, and the batsman has to refocus and begin concentrating once again. Most rain interruptions produce a wicket and it was no different this time as Pollock found the edge of Porty's bat. The all-too familiar pattern of our batsmen getting starts and not going on continued. Besides JB's duck, our top six scores ranged from 14 to 30. DLS came in at the end and hit a maximum but we knew our score of 152 off 35 overs was probably not enough.

Because of all the interruptions the hour-long break was reduced to ten minutes. And because I was still being bound up with all the tape my body needs to stay together these days, I missed the first over of their innings. But I knew something special had happened when I heard the roar from the crowd and Adi shouting: 'You beauty!' Boyd's third ball of the innings to AB De Villiers was caught by Porty at backward point. It was another great start. My opposite number, Graeme Smith, put together a good partnership with Jacques Kallis, who had been in incredible form in the competition. Paul Mooney came on and was desperately unlucky not to get a wicket with his first ball. Kallis played a thick inside edge that just missed the stumps and went through Niall's legs for four. Smith then lobbed one over my head, but I finally removed him when he went legside to give himself some room and hit it back to me. I took a low catch to my right, and was up like a flash to start the Chicken Dance. But we struggled with Jacques Kallis: you don't score 10,000 ODI runs without being a truly great player. Gibbs came in and didn't last long and became Boyd's second victim of the day to a good catch by Andy, but Kallis brought the South Africans home with 3.3 overs left.

After the press conference was over we sat down with our new friends and talked the talk. The South African guys are very decent and down to earth, especially big Andre Nel. Still, when I looked around our dressing room afterwards I saw the disappointment in the players' faces, which was good to see. We had improved some aspects of our game, too. We were destroyed by the South Africans' death bowling in the warm-up game in Trinidad, but in Providence we managed to clear the fence a few times.

With six days to our next game we were given a welcome day off, which I made the most of to get some intensive work on my shoulder. In my heart I knew that it was still not right, but the memory of sitting in the stands while the guys battled the West Indies was fresh and raw, and I would have done anything to stay on the park. I sat in my room constructing my weekly column for the Irish newspaper, the *Sunday Independent*, when the phone rang. It was Paul Mooney telling me the guys were going down to the popular Windies Bar to watch the England v Sri Lanka game followed by Manchester United. I took up their offer after my newspaper piece was complete. Unfortunately for Paul, Porty and Roy Torrens, Man U went down 2-1 to Roma so there was no mood for celebration and an early night followed.

There was a sense of excitement brewing the next morning, though, as we finally got to do something other than cricket or sleep. It was a tough seventeen days in Guyana with not a lot to do. The pride of the country is the Kaieteur Falls, an enormous waterfall that is a must-see for visitors. At Cheddi Jagan International Airport in Georgetown we were split into three groups of six and weighed individually before being allocated our tiny planes. These things are not my cup of tea and there were a few sideways glances as Porty, Paul, Andre, Big Phil Simmons, the pilot and myself hopped on board and headed for the runway. I must confess to being really nervous at that moment and as I looked around the tiny plane it was obvious that I was not alone. The plane was guided by a Global Positioning System similar to one you might have in a car. I thought of mum and all those times she tried to get me to go to church with her. The flight took fifty minutes – and we couldn't wait to touch earth. One of the planes was delayed by fog and turned up thirty minutes late, so our experience could have been worse.

Kaieteur Falls is on the Potara River in central Guyana and located in the Kaieteur National Park, a region that is claimed by Venezuela. It is the largest single drop waterfall in the world, a 226m sheer descent that produces a thunderous noise before you even reach it. The volume of water that roars over the sandstone is an unbelievable 650,000 litres per second. It is five times higher than Niagara Falls and about twice the height of Victoria Falls. The Sky Sports News team joined us for the day –

they had been excellent for raising the profile of the sport back home – and Adam Leventhal gave me the microphone to do a few interviews with the guys. While I was a bit nervous at first, it soon flowed quite smoothly. We then got back into our flying shoebox to travel to Baganara Island, the largest of the 365 islands in the mighty Essequibo River. This little paradise was a wonderful venue for lunch and some well-needed chill time. Paul Mooney went wakeboarding while the rest of us took it easy but that all ended with a competitive game of volleyball. That outing taught me one important lesson: if Peter Johnston is around and you're playing volleyball, make sure he's on the other team.

After two days away from cricket, Adi was keen to push us to the limits and that's what happened the next morning in Everest. We started with our normal game of touch rugby (won by the Youngies), before the bowlers had a 10 to 12 over workout and the batsmen a good stint in the nets. The local cricket clubs provided us with net bowlers, youngsters who would come and bowl all day and give us a good going over. It was great for us that these were such quality players. However, the wickets at the club were slowly getting worse, due to the wear and tear of the daily practise sessions and we requested permission to train at the Providence Stadium.

New Zealand were our last opponents in Guyana – a good, well-coached team. Adi and I sat down after training and chatted about selection and our opponents. We wondered how much better than us they would be if you were to take their fast bowler, Shane Bond, out of the equation. They've got a good spinner, Daniel Vettori; we've got a good spinner in Kyle McCallan. They've got bowlers who bowl at 130kph; we've got bowlers who bowl at 130kph. They're a good fielding side; we're a good fielding side. They've good quality batsmen – they wouldn't be the team they are if they hadn't. But we have good quality batsmen too. The difference is that they are professional. They play cricket all the time. We can't say we'll go out and beat them, but we will be competitive. And then again, if we play out of our skins and they have a shocker, who knows?

Training on Saturday was in the afternoon, so we were given the morning off. I spent the time with Knoxy working on my shoulder. The nets are right behind the players' stand, so training was difficult as there was a game being played inside the stadium between Bangladesh and South Africa. We had a good hit out with bat and ball before travelling back to the hotel. Adi and I went back to watch the second half of the game and it turned out not to be the result Ireland – or our bank balance – was looking for. South Africa were squeezed by the three left-arm spinners of Bangladesh, and they were bowled out 67 runs short of the target. Bangladesh now had two points in the Super Eights and we now needed to not just beat them, but have a better run-rate too, to finish seventh. The ICC prize fund allocated $50,000 to eighth place, but that doubled to $100,000 for seventh. With all the players losing out financially to represent their country, that extra $50,000 – about €40,000 – would be a great help.

On Saturday night we went to a boxing match: Guyanese style. It was an open air event at the National Park and has been hyped as The Conclusion. Adi, Matt, Paul, Kenny, Andre and myself made the trip and had a hell of a night. There were five bouts altogether including a women's fight, and the main event between Andrew 'Six Heads' Lewis, a former world welterweight champion, and 'Deadly' Danny Dalton. It was one night I would have liked Frank, our police escort, with us, as there were people of all shapes and sizes there and at times it was quite daunting. We had great ringside seats and discovered we were next to Six Heads' brothers, who were crazy dudes indeed. His fight went the distance but Six Heads came out on top on points. A lovely policewoman arranged a cab for us and we finally left The Conclusion at 1.30am on Sunday morning.

Luckily enough we had a light session the next morning in preparation for the game against the Kiwis. The Oldies were victorious in the rugby before we got down to the serious business. We had been struggling with our 'death' bowling, so the bowlers were asked to bowl in two spells to get them used to coming back on. Some of us bowled four overs, a break, then two; others went three, break, three.

We returned to the Cara Lodge for a quick shower and change before spending the afternoon with some people less fortunate than us. Nine members of the party visited a shelter housing for fourteen children who, until a few weeks before, were living rough on the streets of Georgetown. The shelter was the brainchild of Mrs Varshire Jagdeo, Guyana's First Lady. These kids had either run away or been thrown out onto the streets by their families. At the shelter they received care and got food and an education. We played cricket with them and gave them some lollies. I left Mrs Jagdeo one of my shirts for her to auction and raise some money. Our next stop was to a local hospital in Georgetown and the children's paediatric department. Again it was another moving experience. We walked around and spoke to the children and their parents. We again gave the kids some lollies and biscuits and for only a small part of their day we put a smile on those faces. At the end of our ninety-minute trip we made a small donation to another charity the First Lady works with, the 'Heart to Heart Save a Life Appeal'. This organisation takes twenty children from families who can't afford treatment, and brings them to India for heart surgery, which costs US$55,000 (€40,000) a time. The players and the Irish Cricket Union made a donation, which Roy presented to Mrs Jagdeo. The big guy did very well with all the emotion floating around the place. He said: 'Thousands of people are coming to watch us play cricket, and treating us like heroes, but it is you, Mrs Jagdeo, and the children we have seen who are the real heroes. Today, cricket seems very insignificant.' He hit it right on the button.

In the build-up to our next game against New Zealand there were a few injury and selection problems. Andre was ruled out of the team for the next match after tweaking his hamstring, so Kevin came back into the side. The pitch looked flatter than that for the South African game so we expected to use Andy White more than a seamer and we went for the extra bat, with Peter Gillespie brought in for Paul Mooney. It was Peter's first game of the competition and everyone was delighted for him. Polish is a hugely popular member of our group. Yet again, I lost the toss and it was no surprise when New Zealand elected to bat. They got off to a pretty good start but we took wickets regularly. Big Boyd claimed another prize scalp in their captain, Stephen Fleming, who fell to a top-class catch at backward point by Porty. Hamish Marshall, Scott Styris and Craig McMillan all came and went and when I checked the scoreboard New Zealand were 118 for four – exactly the same situation we had with England ten days earlier. DLS finally got to bring the Ferret Dance out in Guyana, and he bowled well, considering he hadn't strayed far from a toilet over the previous four days, a bad case of food poisoning. Once again we were unstuck by lower order batsman with good eyes and equally good records. James Franklin was batting nine, and he has a test match hundred and a first class double hundred to his name. He and Brendon McCullum went to town on us in the last six overs and they posted a daunting 260. With Bond and their two spinners, Vettori and Patel, in form it was going to be a tough task.

Once again JB was out early. Jeremy is never one that believes he is ever out on merit – he either gets a brute of a delivery or the wicket is crap. This time he did get a good ball, one that pitched outside leg, went across him and he got a tickle, which was taken by McCullum in front of first slip. Once again Porty and Morgan looked to be building a solid partnership when both got out too early and we were 35 for three. The O'Brien brothers came together but Niall struggled a little early on. Kevin unloaded some big hits and with their partnership, worth 75, they were looking good. Unfortunately, a mix-up over a run ended their stand and it all went downhill from there. Kevin was run out for 49 and Niall went soon after for 30, but the last six wickets fell for the addition of just nine runs and we were all out for 134.

It was the same story in two out of the three games in Guyana – we let it slip for five or ten overs and that was enough for the top sides to put us away. The press conference went well, no real tough questions, just another day of learning our trade at this level.

11 THE HOME FRONT

The victory over Pakistan came on the same day, 17 March 2007, as Ireland's rugby players narrowly lost the Six Nations championship title to France. And as a result, many newspapers contrasted the highs and lows of the travelling fans in Rome and Jamaica. But the Irish love winners and the rugby defeat was rapidly consigned to history, as the whole island took to this thrilling new sport and its marvellous representatives. Politicians clambered to congratulate the team and newspapers published guides to the game for newcomers. Pubs where the sole topic of conversation had been Mourinho v Ferguson echoed to discussion of 'powerplays' and 'inswinging yorkers'.

The team received letters of congratulations from the Taoiseach, Bertie Ahern, and President, Mary McAleese, and later received a remarkable letter from the First, Rev Ian Paisley, and Deputy First Minister, Martin McGuinness, at Stormont. Political progress had been made in the weeks leading up to the World Cup, but it was still a cause of surprise and delight to read the previously implacable enemies uniting in support of the cricketers. 'This is a marvellous achievement. I warmly congratulate the team and pay particular tribute to the Northern Ireland players and their manager, Ulsterman, Roy Torrens,' wrote Ian Paisley, 'Qualifying for the tournament itself was tremendous, but making the Super Eight stage was nothing short of remarkable.' Sinn Fein vice-president, Martin McGuinness, said: 'Irish teams and their supporters are world renowned for their willingness to celebrate our sporting successes. When these are achieved against the odds and confound all expectations it makes them all the sweeter. I am particularly delighted to have seen the contribution made to the team's success of local players: Jeremy Bray, Peter Gillespie, Kyle McCallan and Andrew White.' While McGuinness got his facts wrong – he left out Boyd Rankin and William Porterfield and his inclusion of Sydneysider, Jeremy Bray, stretched the definition of 'local' – his comments were well received by the team. McGuinness is a long-time fan of the game and reportedly watched much of the 2005 Ashes. He was reported as being 'devastated' not to have been able to meet his hero, Andrew Flintoff, when the player came to Belfast to open a call centre, when he played hurling with some Antrim players.

The postal service in the south, An Post, were so delighted with the team – and the involvement of one of their employees, Kenny Carroll – that they announced they would deliver messages of support to the team free of charge. More than 10,000 letters and postcards were sent, and finally delivered to the team when they reached Grenada. This was a fabulous indicator of how the team had found a new wave of supporters, with many letters coming from areas in the country where it had been many years since a set of stumps had been erected. Whole schools sent messages to their heroes and the players were conscientious in reading every single one, and replying to as many as they could. In Barbados, Carroll got to discuss letterbox techniques with Brad Hogg, the spin-bowler who was a postman himself and is still employed by the Australian Post Office.

This fact that most of the country was discovering the game for the first time was in some ways an indictment of the stewardship of the Irish Cricket Union. Most grounds in Ireland are hidden from public view, buried in urban areas behind rows of houses. It can be hard to turn a casual interest in the game into active participation, but this will become a challenge the union will have to meet if the sport is to move to a new level. The raw material was certainly there after the World Cup. Trent Johnston's mantra at press conferences was that his main aim in the

Caribbean was to show the world that Ireland had a good cricket team, and also to spread the word back home – on both counts the campaign was an outstanding success.

Several players had laptop computers and kept in touch with what has happening back home, all the positive and supportive footage helped keep them focused. They heard about the St Patrick's Night céilí that was cancelled in a County Kerry GAA club because the men wouldn't leave the bar as victory over Pakistan was slowly secured. They heard about the last race being delayed at Shelbourne Park greyhound track because the big screen was showing the climax of that game – a particular delight to Ginger O'Brien, a regular at the dog track and father of Kevin and Niall. They also watched the YouTube video website and were astonished to see the footage from Clohessy's Bar in Limerick. The south-western city is a hotbed of sport, particularly rugby, but contains just one small cricket club. The bar's owner, Peter Clohessy, was a much-capped rugby international of the 1990s and his vast Howley's Quay premises is a popular spot in the city. The YouTube video showed the reaction of the crowd to Johnston's match-winning six against Pakistan – as far as the eye can see there were people leaping in the air and screaming with delight.

The Taoiseach, Bertie Ahern, had never previously shown any interest in the summer game, although he wore his heart on his Manchester United and Dublin GAA shirt sleeves at every opportunity. Popping in for his nightly pint in Fagan's of Drumcondra on St Patrick's Day, he was astonished to see every television set in the pub tuned to Sky Sports and the action in Sabina Park, and all eyes on them. The election plotting was put aside for an hour as the game reached its thrilling climax and Ahern cheered and roared with the best of them. He spoke the next day about his pride in the players and his surprise at how they had captured the imagination in places like Fagan's, where premiership and Croke Park matters usually held sway. The famous GAA venue was invoked several times, with *Irish Examiner* columnist,

Michael Moynihan, suggesting that cricket be staged there next.

The Ian Dempsey radio show on Today FM features a popular comedy slot each day called 'Gift Grub'. Several times during the World Cup its creator, Mario Rosenstock, turned his wit on cricket, lampooning Ahern's new-found passion, 'Cricket's a lot like the health service – dere's a lot of waiting around and no one seems sure how it works', and composing two songs inspired by the event. The *Gift* Ronan Keating sang a *Can We Cricket?* rap, while there was a masterful spoof of *Joxer Goes to Stuttgart*, Christy Moore's ode to the soccer fan at Euro '88. *Roger Goes to Guyana* played to the old prejudices about cricket's upper-class profile, but was still a big hit with players and fans:

It was in the year '07, in a place that was very warm,
That the Irish cricket team, took the world by storm
So when we headed for Guyana, our hearts were full of pride
Roger packed his platinum visa and set out from Malahide.

From Killiney, Howth and Sutton, Clontarf, Dalkey we all flew
On business class with Aer Lingus, cos we're fairly well to do
And by the time we hit Barbados, the lads were fairly jarred
All that vintage champagne; said Roger 'Put it on my card!'

The next day when we woke up, our heads were full of pain
But it never feels quite as bad, waking up in Sandy Lane
We all met up in the foyer, for Guyana we were set,
All except for Roger who went by private jet.

That day against the English, no one gave us half a chance
They all said Freddie Flintoff, would lead us a merry dance
But for Michael Vaughan and Pietersen, it all went pretty sour
When the Irish fast bowlers bowled them out in half an hour.

What followed next was legendary, 'twas an historic day
We won by seven wickets, and a hundred for Jeremy Bray
The last time we saw Roger he was off to party hard

Arm in arm with Trent Johnston saying 'stick it on the card!'
(©Mario Rosenstock, 'Gift Grub', on the Ian Dempsey Breakfast Show)

The Irish Times carried an extraordinary letter from a Pakistani who was clearly upset at his nation's defeat, but had a dubious solution to its woes: 'Madam, I am a blue-blooded Pakistani with a lot of love of your countrymen. You deserved every bit of the victory in Jamaica. You played for the love of the game and the love of your country. I would gladly have the behind of my country brutalised by the Irish any day. Perhaps this way some of your qualities can rub off them.' Yours, etc., Isfandyar Khan, Islamabad, Pakistan.

Those Irish cricket supporters unlucky not to have been in Jamaica flew the flag strongly, and the likes of the Russell Court Hotel in Dublin, several club bars and the Merry Cricketer in Balrothery, were frequently visited by reporters and camera crews. The Merry Cricketer had to close its doors at times and fans resorted to looking through the windows to catch a glimpse of the game. Tommy Mooney talked to Conor McMorrow of the *Sunday Tribune*: 'I never thought I would see the day when my two nephews would be playing in the World Cup. This is a very special time for me as my brother, John 'the Ranger' Mooney, was their father and he passed away a few years ago. He was a fantastic player with North County and he would be so proud of them if he was here today. All Irish people should be happy for this cricket team.'

One area where supply couldn't keep pace with demand was in the market for replica shirts. Kukri sent several hundred units to the shops in January, but they were all sold by the time the competition started. After the Pakistan game there was a surge of demand, which was unable to be met because of a six-week turn around time at the manufacturers. 'We've been inundated with enquiries up to a hundred phone calls a day,' said John Larkin of Elvery's in Dublin. 'The main demand has been for shirts. We could have sold thousands but we can't get them.' This was an extraordinary development, as the ICU usually struggle to get 1,000 paying customers through the gates for home games, although matches against the likes of England, Australia and West Indies would attract many more.

The fans were back in force for the Barbados leg of the competition, with many availing of the island's more tourist-friendly location and facilities. Many Irish supporters signed up for a week-long cruise that sailed every evening between the islands of Barbados and Grenada, depositing them each morning in time for a Super Eights game. An estimated 1,500 Irish fans turned up in Bridgetown, with many coming down from the US and Canada – where word had spread of their success. The Blarney Army were augmented by the overwhelming majority of Bajans. The Irish team's spirit and sense of joy had captured the locals wherever they visited and the extra support proved useful at the Kensington Oval. The ICC had attracted criticism over its ticket prices – the cheapest seat in Guyana was US$25, about half the average weekly wage. The absence of Pakistan and, particularly, India hit the tourism targets and many seats at 'sell-out' games went unused. The ICC responded by opening the gates to all, after an hour's play, which helped recapture some of the party atmosphere missing from much of the tournament. *The Nation* newspaper reported: 'Most demonstrable in support of the Irish are the Barbadian spectators. Spectators packed the Party Stand to cheer the Irish with drums, whistles, and trumpets – buoying the Irish on to a shocking upset of Bangladesh. Enthusiastic fans and cheerful cricketers were doing the 'Chicken Dance', Johnston's little jig, and Dave Langford-Smith's 'Ferret Dance', captured the imagination of many, and their footwork was copied across many dance floors and playgrounds all over the world in the following weeks.

Every move the Irish team made, on dance floors or cricket stadiums, was captured by two indefatigable film-makers. Ed Leahy of RTÉ was working on a general film about cricket in Ireland, to be shown in 2008, while independent film-maker, Paul Davey, was trying to capture the magic of the Caribbean adventure, for televising at Christmas 2007. Sligoman, Davey had been jogging in a Sydney park, in early 2006, when he saw a fellow runner wearing an Irish jersey. He stopped to chat to the jogger, who turned out to be Niall O'Brien. Their encounter turned out to be one of those serendipitous meetings which change lives. Davey was unaware of Ireland's cricket team and was even more surprised to hear that they had qualified for the forthcoming World Cup. A plan hatched in his head and the young film-maker headed for Jamaica, for what he thought would be a fortnight. Instead his short film turned into an epic seven-week tale. Davey arranged with the ICU for unprecedented access to the team, and physio, Iain Knox, took the camera into places where film-makers aren't allowed. They captured some extraordinary dressing room moments including Trent Johnston's speech before the last session against Pakistan, and Peter Gillespie's hilarious miming of Ed Joyce letting a Rankin delivery knock his stumps over. But the night before the Irish team was due to fly to Guyana for the Super Eights, Davey was tearing his hair out because he simply didn't have the cash to get there. He was about to cry into his beer, when he was approached by David Hall, the Jamaican head of Digicel. Hall told him that the company's chief executive, Denis O'Brien, had heard of his plight and offered to fund his flights and accommodation for the rest of the adventure, allowing him to complete his project, no strings attached.

Most of the players' wives and girlfriends had been in Jamaica, and a few were able to return for the short Barbados leg. The term WAGs had been coined by the UK media for the group of dazzling women, many ex-popstars and models, who partnered members of the England soccer team at the 2006 World Cup. A lot of the UK media reported on the WAGs activities; grabbing headlines and filling pages upon pages of photographs of their outfits. As a result, subsequent sporting events paid enormous attention to partners and spouses – such as the Ryder Cup and Ashes tour. The first inkling that this might apply to them hit the Irish women the weekend before the World Cup, when Ydele Steele, Andrew White's fiancée, was the subject of a full-page interview in the *Sunday Life* newspaper. In the Caribbean they were regularly shown on TV screens and featured in the press, which bemused some of them. 'I don't object to the term WAGs but I wouldn't use it for us,' said Ciara Gillespie, wife of Peter. 'It just goes way over my head. We just have a good laugh about it. Posh Spice? I'm the complete opposite!'

JM Barrie, author of *Peter Pan*, was himself a keen cricketer. He once wrote that: 'Having a good wife is like scoring 50 at cricket. In fact, having a good wife is like scoring 99. But beyond that I will not go.' Having a cricket wife is just about the dream partner for Peter Gillespie. 'I've been brought up with cricket through my ancestors,' Ciara told the *Sunday Tribune*. 'It's always been cricket through both sides of my family. Tommy Gallagher, of Sion Mills, was my grandfather. On my mother's side, I'm descended from Andy McFarlane.' (One of the greatest batsmen ever to play for Ireland.) 'There isn't much women's cricket in the north-west, so I have never played it, but I really understand it well since I started going out with Peter. Back then I never enjoyed watching it. It was boring.' The pair first met at Strabane CC in 2001 and were married in September 2006 – and gave up their honeymoon to allow him to prepare for the World Cup. 'We were planning to get a few extra days in Jamaica after the cricket was over but the way things worked out we got a lot more time together.'

Trent Johnston's wife, Vanessa, played the game at first team level for Trinity and Leinster, 'But my sport has definitely had to take a back seat due to Trent's cricket and the kids, but I coach under tens hockey now which I enjoy,' she says. Claudia (seven) plays with Railway Union under nines while Charlie (four) is more of a rugby tot.

Coach Adrian Birrell's wife, Susan, was a cricket nut from an early age. 'I was a keen supporter of the local games at St George's in Port Elizabeth,' she said. 'I was one of the fanatical ones who queued at 4.00am to get tickets for those rebel tours that came to South Africa. I remember sitting there with our chairs and picnic baskets. We were quite avid.' Susan had to sacrifice a lot to watch her husband fulfil his dream. A chartered accountant, she was a partner in Deloitte and

Above: England all-rounder, Freddie Flintoff, enjoys capturing the wicket of DLS.

Below: Paul Mooney has a sympathetic word for Ed Joyce at the end of the game in Georgetown.

Above: Roy Torrens and our new friends in the Georgetown orphanage.

Below: Trent Johnston and Paul Mooney get close to the edge at Kaieteur.

Above: Team meeting in the Cara Lodge in Georgetown.

Below: Spin quartet Matt Dwyer, Kyle McCallan, Lance Gibbs and Andrew White in the Bourda.

Above: Ready to tee off in Sandy Lane were Peter Gillespie, Iain Knox, Adi Birrell and Trent Johnston.

Below: The Blarney Army regrouped in Barbados - Colm Rainey, Dermot Rainey, Peter Gallagher, Iain Ferguson and Stephen Kerr.

Above: Trent despatches player of the tournament, Glenn McGrath, for four.

Below: Maebh Langford-Smith, Lynne McCallan, Ydele Steele and Vanessa Johnston relaxing in Ocho Rios.

Those peculiar specimens of Irish wildlife, the 'chicken dance' (above) and 'funky ferret' (below) went down a bomb in Barbados.

Above: Adi Birrell with West Indies captain Brian Lara.

Below: Taoiseach Bertie Ahern tries on the jersey with Trent and Adi.

Back: Matt Dywer, Iain Knox, Kenny Carroll, John Mooney, Jeremy Bray, Boyd Rankin, Andre Botha, Kevin O'Brien, Paul Mooney, Pete Johnston, Roy Torrens.

Front: Niall O'Brien, William Porterfield, Andrew White, Eoin Morgan, Trent Johnston, Adrian Birrell, Kyle McCallan, Peter Gillespie, Dave Langford-Smith.

Touche in South Africa, when Birrell was considering applying for the job of coaching Ireland. 'I did tell him to think long and hard about it,' she says, 'just because I knew it would be a big commitment. But it was the logical next step for him. He had been coaching Eastern Province for three years and was at a kind of crossroads. I said, '"go for it and we'll see what happens." And he was successful, so we moved! I decided that there was probably more opportunity for me to advance my career at a later stage than Adrian. It would be a lot easier for me to get back into it than he would. I did have one little condition, though, when he was offered the job with Ireland. I said he could only take it if I could arrange a transfer with my firm.' With their first son Luke (eight), the Birrells took the long trek north to Malahide, County Dublin. Susan joined the Irish division of Deloitte and Touche and late in 2006 was again promoted to partner. With the World Cup providing a natural full stop to Adrian's tenure as coach, he announced that he would step down after the adventure was over. With two lively sons (Christopher was born in Dublin in 2005) 'it is always a balancing act,' she explained. 'It is one of the factors that Adrian considered when he resigned from the Ireland job. We both travel a lot with our jobs, which is difficult when it comes to managing the children. A decision was taken that as I was made partner in Dublin that I would need to focus on my career for a while. He's going to stay in cricket in some way but more to facilitate our sons as I did.' Ireland's unexpected success meant the Birrell's post-Jamaica family holiday in Mexico had to be aborted, with a fortnight in Guyana not quite ideal for a young family.

Vanessa Johnston, too, had to make huge sacrifices in her life with Trent. 'We had a five-day honeymoon during a Saturday/Saturday two-day game. Trent was away for our first five wedding anniversaries, and when I found out that I was pregnant with Claudia. My father-in-law brought me home from hospital with Charlie. But Trent is the man I first met in 1995, and I always knew that sport would be an important part of his life, and it is an important part of who he is. The first year back in

Ireland was very hard. TJ had a job lined up which fell through; I was working for Nestlé and he was at home looking after the kids. The only thing that really went to plan was the cricket. Looking back I wouldn't change a thing and what doesn't kill you makes you stronger. We are stronger for the shared experience.' Trent now works for Architectural Hardware and Vanessa is still with Nestlé. Having spent a fortnight in Jamaica with the children, Vanessa was delighted that her parents and friends volunteered to mind the children, so she could go to Barbados. The support and commitment of cricket wives and partners is greatly appreciated, not just by the team, but also the management, crew and fans, especially now that yet another magical week was about to happen as the Irish cricket team stepped onto the rollercoaster once again.

12 THE FINAL SESSION

We arrived in Barbados on 10 April 2007, and looming large at the end of that week was an exciting – if daunting – prospect. In three days I was due to play against the country of my birth: Australia – the reigning champions and a team that hadn't lost a World Cup match to anyone for eight years!

To be honest, it was a relief to finally leave Guyana. The eighteen days that we had spent there had taken its toll on the guys and we were all eagerly awaiting our stay at the Bridgetown Hilton. Vanessa was also coming to Barbados for ten days, so I was looking forward to being able to share this stage of the competition with her. It had always been our journey – she had sacrificed a lot for me to achieve this dream. I was happy that my children were enjoying being at home with my in-laws.

The first two and half days in Barbados went by in a flash. Training anchored every day, and Adi and I spent a great deal of time working out how to compete against this in-form and ruthless Australian team. We trained at the 3W's ground (named after the West Indian legends of the 1950s and '60s: Everton Weekes, Frank Worrell and Clyde Walcott), where the wickets were a lot quicker with more bounce than they had been in Guyana. A few of our net bowlers took advantage of this and hit the gloves and upper body of a few of our batsmen. Boyd even managed to fire up the usually calm Niall O'Brien with a couple of short balls that rapped him on the gloves. Coming from the slow, low wickets in Guyana we bowlers enjoyed that particular session.

We also had our first taste of Kensington Oval, one of the great grounds of the world. The redevelopment programme of the grounds had produced a spectacular venue. We had an opportunity to train on the outfield and survey the ground, but I already knew which end I would be bowling from come Friday – The Malcolm Marshall End. As I mentioned previously, I had been a huge Marshall fan as a boy – he was everything I wanted to be in a cricketer. I really felt that something special could happen here over the next four days. The hard work had been done and now it was time to prepare mentally.

With Vanessa now in Barbados I had a chance to relax before the big day against the Aussies. I had played with the England batsman, Andrew Strauss at Mosman, and we had become great friends with him and his wife, Ruth. We had kept in touch over the years and were delighted when it emerged that we would all have time to catch up in Barbados. Whilst Andy and the English team were compiling a win against Bangladesh at Kensington Oval, we were making sandcastles on the beach with Ruth and their little boy, Samuel. I really missed Claudia and Charlie and thought about the fact that I really hadn't been able to spend much time together in Jamaica – given the distance between Kingston and Ocho Rios. I had been away from home for such a long time; I thought of my children and the next time we would all be together. That night the Strausses and Johnstons went out for dinner and I was able to pick Straussy's brains about Bangladesh and Australia. At one stage the conversation even left cricket, which was a nice change.

I'm not a good person to be around before a game, regardless of the opposition, and on the eve of the encounter with the champions my head was in a spin. Could we possibly stop them? Would we compete? Or was it going to be the result that all the pundits were expecting? At the team meeting everyone seemed reasonably relaxed, John Boy was picked to come in for the still-injured Andre, but other than that we were at full strength. I talked to Adi that night, and we wondered if they would rest some key players or mix their batting and bowling line-ups. Kevin Pietersen, the England batsman, texted Adi to offer to talk to us about the dos and don'ts of playing Australia. Unfortunately, Adi got the message too late and was not able to respond in time. For a player of Pietersen's stature to offer his services was a mighty gesture and, in hindsight, I think it would really have benefited us.

The media attention became more intense for me as well. It was difficult at times – I'd never been in that situation before, although I don't think it affected my performance, it did add extra pressure. When things kicked off like they did in the first two games, it went through the roof and I had people ringing me at all hours. I don't know how the big boys do it. We were a bit innocent and didn't have a code of conduct with the hotel who kept putting calls through day and night. I think I missed an awful lot of these, though, because the lobby would put them through to Pete Johnston our video analyst. Pete's voice is now extremely well known in some strange parts of the world! But a huge part of what we wanted to achieve at the World Cup was to raise the profile of Irish cricket so I did everything I was asked. I knew it was something that I had to do.

There was a radio station in Melbourne that used to ring me nearly every night on its sports programme, 'The Good Oil'. It was presented by former test cricketer, Rodney Hogg, and netball champion, Sharelle McMahon. I got into the banter and they were delighted when I was able to quote their finest hours back at them. But I probably shouldn't have because they couldn't get enough of me for the next month, to the serious detriment of my sleeping patterns.

Vee knows that on the morning of any game it's best just to wish me luck and then leave me alone. In the hotel, she even sat at another table for breakfast. As we arrived at the ground I was both nervous and excited. I had Paddy Casey running through my iPod, which calms me and pumps me up at the same time. Before the warm ups we discussed how important it was that we enjoyed the day, entertained the crowd and gave the Aussies a real fight. It was also the first time since Jamaica that the Irish supporters were back in numbers. During the warm-ups I noticed that it was my old friend, Stuart Clark, marking out his run up – so the Australians were obviously making a change. Could they be resting their fastest bowler, Shaun Tait? No such luck. In fact it was Nathan Bracken who they had sidelined. This really did not effect our preparations because deep down I knew Ricky Ponting and the Australians wanted to put us to the sword and show the gap that was between the two cricketing countries.

The toss was won by Ponting and – to the crowd's obvious displeasure – he elected to bowl. That reaction really angered me. Had I won the toss we would have batted anyway – let us be honest if we scored 170 and were beaten by eight or nine wickets we would have done well. But if they had batted and got 400 and rolled us for a hundred it would have been described as a farce. I spoke to the guys before we started and told them we had to show this crowd we could play, be competitive and belong on this stage.

It didn't start well at all. The first ball of the game saw Tait bowl what was later described by some Aussie players as the quickest ball they have seen in any form of cricket. Just the noise of the ball hitting Adam Gilchrist's gloves sent a shiver through the camp. Soon we were four wickets down for 12 and starring down the barrel of a thrashing. With the help of 15 wides, Kevin, John Boy and I got us to a scratchy total of 91. It was simply awesome to face Glenn McGrath and Tait. I even managed to take ten off one over from the old man of Australia cricket, McGrath, who was the eventual player of the tournament. The thrill of this didn't last long though, as Tait then came on and bowled four balls that didn't even register on my line of vision. I played the fourth of them onto my stumps and my innings was over. The only consolation was that we got past the lowest World Cup scores of Scotland, Namibia and Canada.

At the ten minutes innings break, we spoke about salvaging some pride and giving our supporters something to take home. Who would open the batting for them? How long could we keep them out there for?

Could we trouble them? Adam Gilchrist and Michael Hussey came out, and as they hadn't shown much form in the tournament, we knew we had an opportunity to get a couple of wickets at least. Their class came to the fore, however, and they got off to a flyer. I mixed our bowling up in the hope we might get one or two wickets. In the end, we got just one, when I bowled Gilly from around the wicket with a pretty good ball – from the Malcolm Marshall end too. It gave me a chance to unleash the, by-now crowd favourite, Chicken Dance once again. But Andrew Symonds then came out and in no time we were back in the sheds for the post-mortem.

It was important that we keep it in perspective – we had just been beaten by a team that had been the best in the world for nearly fifteen years. Due to their punishing schedule, the Australians spend thirty nights a year in their own beds; we would be lucky to spend thirty days together as a squad. The press conference wasn't as bad as I had anticipated – I think the press never expected us to challenge them, which in some ways this made the outcome easier to stomach. We spent a bit of time with the Aussie players and got a couple of bats signed for the souvenir cabinet, and I swapped one of my remaining shirts with Adam Gilchrist.

As captain, I knew that it fell to me to lift the team morale in time for our next match – a crucial encounter against Bangladesh two days later. Adi, Matt and I had a good chat and together we devised a plan. Reviewing the flow of our games against Australia and England's victory over Bangladesh, we knew that I had to win the toss and bat first. We had an early start the next day at the Kensington Oval, with little time to get over the humbling we had received the day before. The team had another early night, but some of the girls decided to paint the town red. Their theory was that it would bring the guys luck, which would also mean a precedent could be set. By all accounts (and they were sketchy) a good night was had by all.

Adi had managed to track down Kevin Pietersen, who agreed to chat to us about our last two opponents, Bangladesh and Sri Lanka. It was great to hear how he personally prepared to face these bowlers. He also spoke about how he and the England team would sweep certain spinners, but play straight against others. It was one of the best team talks I have ever had, and as it turned out it really helped the next day. As a player Pietersen divides opinion, but he rose hugely in my estimation for the time he gave us in Barbados.

The morning came and there was a feeling that we had to turn things around. We had held our own and been competitive in the Super Eights – until two days before – but we knew that we couldn't live forever on the success in Sabina Park. We couldn't allow people to say that it had been a once-off. We had a huge boost with the return of Andre, but that meant another difficult selection call. Andy White had been concussed by a Glenn McGrath bouncer, so we wanted to give him as much time as possible to recover, which meant the final decision was left to the morning of the game. Adi, Matt and I concluded that Andy should keep his place, which meant John Boy would miss out. I spoke to John Boy, one-on-one, and could tell that he was hurting – particularly after his heroics against Australia – but he took it on the chin. The Mooneys are team men through and through, and while neither of them had been first choice throughout the tournament (although John was always very close), they were behind us every step of the way. On top of that they have the best travelling supporters – whether their boys were in the starting eleven or not, Frances and the clan were in the stand, cheering on Ireland.

Things continued to fall our way: the Bangladesh opening bowler, Syed Rasel, twisted an ankle in the warm-up and was forced to pull out, and I finally won another toss. We knew that if we could post a score we would be competitive. Our decision to bat was regarded as a strange decision by some, but it was based on they way in which Bangladesh had squeezed England with their three spinners. We knew that we had struggled against spin in this tournament and we knew that we had to take the game to them as this pitch was only going to get slower. JB and William had had a poor series of opening stands in the tournament – 0, 7, 3, 6, 0, 5 and 2 – but we never doubted they would come off in the end, and they got us off to the dream start. They took balls on their hands and body, but stood firm. JB was eventually run out with the score on 92. We had seen off the new ball but now had to face the barrage of spin. We batted positively and attacked when necessary, although the four run-outs were a lowlight in a brave batting display. William Porterfield eventually fell for a gutsy and determined 85. Porty probably got his start in the team because of his reputation as a lightning fielder who could open the batting, but by the end of the World Cup I would have him in my team every day of the week. The way his batting came along in the last year was remarkable. He is first in the nets and last to leave, generally with his good mate, Eoin Morgan. This dedication and application to his game has paid off and his two unbeaten hundreds in Kenya were the making of him, while he is undoubtedly in the top ten fielders in the world. After the group stage, Jonathan Agnew of the BBC said Porty was the fielder of the tournament thus far for his superb displays at backward point. His World Cup was characterised by plenty of starts and only one big score, but he has a huge future in the game and the potential to captain his country.

Another one of the young guns stepped up against Bangladesh, with Kevin 'Kiss Me' O'Brien compiling a solid 48, before I managed to run him out, the second time he had fallen that way within sight of a fifty. Mr Muscle is the youngest of the O'Brien clan and a street-wise kid, who is not afraid to mix it with anyone. He has the ability to take the game away from the opposition in a few balls. He came into the side in 2006, stamped his authority immediately and made a brilliant 142 against Kenya in the World League. His most significant innings for Ireland was that day against Pakistan when, with wickets tumbling all around him, Kevin stood firm and guided us home with 16 runs off 52 balls. On that historic day, he proved that not only did he have the mental strength to cope with the pressure, but that he could adapt to any situation. Kevin is a partnership breaker with the ball and if he can apply a little more focus with his bowling, Irish cricket will have a genuine all rounder. Having run Kevin out I owed the team a few runs, and I got 30 quickly including my 14th six of the calendar year in ODIs, and we ended up on 243.

The original seeding had decreed that fixture to be India v Pakistan – an enormous game in any competition – but Ireland and Bangladesh had turned the World Cup on its head. Many Indian fans who had bought tickets were far, far away from their seats that morning, so the ICC opened the gates after ninety minutes play, and by the time Bangladesh came to bat the ground was packed with 15,500 fans – the atmosphere was electric. While we bowled an extra three overs in wides, we attacked and fielded as well as our opposition had two days earlier. With the exception of the European Championships in 2006, this was the best I have seen DLS bowl and his 2-27 was a great reward.

Boyd was unplayable and held the key to us shaking them up. Andre had the dangerous Aftab Ahmed caught behind off another sensational catch. Niall's keeping throughout the World Cup was consistently good and his work up to the stumps was second to none. I, once again, threw the ball to Kyle and he delivered with two wickets. I picked up a couple of wickets and when I bowled my counterpart Habibul Bashar their fate was sealed. Ireland had made it onto the front and back pages world wide again. It was the most complete one-day team performance I saw in the four years I was involved with Irish cricket. It was to be our final lap-of-honour, and we soaked it up for all it was worth.

Some of the Irish fans told me that this was the best game they had ever seen. The nature of the win meant that it was so much more enjoyable than the nail-biting victories in Sabina Park. There were members of the English Barmy Army, led by their main man, Jimmy, who had been assisting the Blarney Army in the musical department. There was a trumpet player who led several renditions of *Molly Malone, The Fields of Athenry* and *Waltzing Matilda*. There were large numbers of Indian and Pakistani supporters, all of whom seemed to have adopted us in spite of their geographical proximity to Bangladesh. I was even asked to sign an Indian playing shirt ... And the huge numbers of locals who had taken us as their own since the early days of the competition were fantastic.

William Porterfield received the Man of the Match award from the legendary Bajan Gordon Greenidge. At the presentation I asked Porty whether he remembered Gordon as a player, to which he replied, 'He bowled heat didn't he?' I explained that Greenidge had in fact *faced* the heat, and was half of one of the greatest opening partnerships in cricket history. If there had been an Effort Award on offer in the 2007 World Cup we would have won hands down for this performance. To turn our game around after the humbling we got from Australia was a sign of this team's desire, passion and real talent. We celebrated in the dressing room after the game and back in the Hilton later that night, with a smaller and more personal group of family and friends.

Our final port of call was Grenada, where we were met on the runway by a group of traditional performers, and at the hotel by two local singers. Their rendition of *Welcome Ireland, Welcome, Welcome to Grenada* was truly hilarious – it became a mantra for the final week of our adventure. The Rex Resort was home to all the teams and it really was a Who's Who of international cricket with the three form teams of the tournament – Australia, New Zealand, and our final opponents, Sri Lanka. The night we arrived I had another chat with Adam Gilchrist. He thought that our game against Bangladesh was compelling viewing, from the spirit of competitiveness to the joy of victory, our lap of honour and seeing Big Charlie, from Strabane, overcome with emotion. He told me there were a few guys in his room watching the game and they had all thoroughly enjoyed it. Adi gave us the first day in Grenada off, which we spent poolside recounting the events of the last four or five days. The intensity of the competition had taken its toll on us, and we were without exception mentally and physically exhausted. But we had to turn our minds to Sri Lanka and another mountain to climb. On Tuesday, 17 April 2007 we were back on deck and as we drove through the roadside cemetery in St George we got our first glimpse of the new Grenada National Stadium. This extraordinary ground was built by the Chinese government as a gift to the people of Grenada – and took six months to build from start to finish. There were 500 Chinese workers toiling on it day and night – they slept in a 250-bed dormitory so you can see how they did it.

Adi was aware the boys needed to rest before our last game, which was his last in charge. The net bowlers were put through their paces and the rest of us sat back. As usual the day before the game we had a press conference, but at the back of my mind was the Snip de Jour Cup. The Youngies had tied the series in Barbados due to some very dodgy refereeing from Knoxy. No one was more pumped for the final game than Paul Mooney and this showed in his performance. Paul won the Man of the Match and Man of the Series awards for his outstanding efforts on the pitch. A true icon of Irish cricket and one of my very good mates, Paul's international career spanned from 1998 through to the end of the World Cup, when he called it a day. He gave his all every single time he walked onto the park and, like his younger brother, has a never say die attitude. It was a shame he couldn't break into the team for more than the one game he played. The one true funny man of the dressing room will be sorely missed by all, none more than me. Paul Mooney won't be there in four years time when the Oldies will look to retain the trophy in the sub-continent – when some of the Youngies will be Oldies of course.

We were all dreading our final team meeting. Adrian Birrell is a very emotional guy, so we knew that this would be tough on him. Adi came into the job in 2003 at a low point in Irish cricket. He moved his family from South Africa to chase the dream of coaching Ireland to a World Cup. He brought solid plans with him and wasn't afraid to make hard decisions. I first met Adi in Malahide and instantly knew that Ireland had a real chance of qualifying for the World Cup; he had such drive and ambition. He is a meticulous planner and had done his preparation for his last team talk. He had hand-written and photocopied his parting words, which he handed out and left the room. He obviously knew that he wouldn't have been able to deliver that final speech, but he also knew that it had to be done for us to prepare properly. Birrell is a true genius and wonderful coach and human being.

We knew that this was our final fling and we were determined to go out fighting. Kenny Carroll got his first chance to play. Kenny was a true giant out in the Caribbean; he was the hardest working member of the squad and really left his mark, even though the scorebooks will tell that he only played one game.

Were Sri Lanka going to rest their big guns again, or were they going to be as ruthless and relentless as the Aussies? I believed they would choose the latter approach. We got off to a great start with JB blitzing the ball to all parts. Unfortunately, he tried to hit Maharoof for one too many boundaries and a collapse followed. Maharoof had come on for the eighth over of the innings and JB immediately hit him for two fours before he was dismissed. Before that over was up, we had lost Andre second ball and Eoin for a goldie. Once their star spinner, Muttiah Muralitharan, came on we lost six wickets for eight runs and were looking fairly pathetic on 54 for nine. David Langford-Smith came to the rescue with some big hitting and we ended up on 77 – it was a disappointing way to finish a great tournament. David comes from a place called Orange in rural New South Wales which is famous for growing apples! He played first grade cricket in Sydney and qualified for Ireland at the start of 2006 through his marriage to Maedbh. His performance at the World Cup against some of the greatest players in the world was tremendous. His ferret celebration dance was enjoyed globally, but a real highlight for me was seeing him hitting Murali for 4. David is a fantastic team man and one of the funniest guys in the dressing room. With a bit more self-belief and confidence, he will open the bowling for Ireland for some time to come.

The scorecard made for poor reading with five ducks lined up in the middle order. I was run out; after I thought my drive had beaten Maharoof in his follow-through, it was a nightmare to see him collect and throw, and the ball deflected off my boot and onto the stumps. Kyle's fourth nought of the tournament put him alongside the South African AB de Villiers, which is something to tell the grandchildren. Boyd got Upal Tharanga in the first over, and David introduced the Funky Ferret to Grenada by getting rid of Kumar Sangakkara, in the process nearly dislocating his knee cap. It was left to Kenny Carroll (AKA Squacko) to bowl our final over to Mahela Jayawardene. Kenny had been one of the five ducks, but he will learn from this, and I am sure will play for Ireland in the next three World Cups. He burst onto the scene due to sheer volume of runs for Railway Union in 2006, when he scored four hundreds and over 1,000 runs in all competitions. Carroll captained the under twenty-threes to the European title, and was later picked for the senior and 'A' squads. 'Squacko' is a talented fielder, with a good arm, lightning speed across the ground and a cool exterior. His left-arm wrist-spin needs more work but if he focuses on improving this, he could win selection as an all-rounder. For a guy who wasn't an automatic selection, Carroll really applied himself and his 100 in South Africa was a sign that he has something to offer Irish cricket for the next ten years.

It was another disappointing display but we didn't feel disgraced. After the Bangladesh game, I was asked who was going to play in the final – I nominated Australia and Sri Lanka. In the end they were the only two teams who taught us a lesson, and they were the ultimate finalists. No shame there. The Sri Lankans finished off my collection of bats, which now stood at eleven. At two and a half pounds each, it was no joke lugging them home with everything else.

It was a pretty emotional dressing room after the game, as we now had to say goodbye not only to Adi, but also to our liaison officer, Maccie, and our close protection officers lead by Frank. Frank and Maccie, were outstanding throughout the tournament and really became part of our squad. We had requested that Donaldson 'the Big D' travel with us throughout the Super Eights but when we were told it would be at our expense – so it was never going to happen. He later took a bullet in a raid in Jamaica but luckily was wearing a bullet-proof vest. One love ...

The tournament was now over for us and the party kicked off big time as we celebrated all that we had achieved over the previous seven weeks. Vanessa had one more day in the Caribbean before she went home. Due to flight scheduling we had to stay for a full weekend in Grenada and Barbados, but unfortunately a big portion of the day after our last game was spent with the Jamaican constabulary investigating the Bob Woolmer case. All the squad were interviewed and gave DNA samples. While we were all happy to assist the enquiry, it was not exactly the way I wanted to spend Vee's last day in the Caribbean. The police visit also meant that I couldn't take part in the Crossbar Challenge, a feature on Sky Sports' 'SoccerAM' show where teams try to hit the bar. My goal-kicking skills would have been useful as we failed to make a mark, although I heard the Boyd hit the crossbar on the second bounce.

It would have been great to be able to go home for one day after the group stages and soak up what was going on back in Ireland. Logistically this would have been impossible, and the travelling would have been detrimental to our performance, but our eventual arrival back at Dublin Airport was incredible. There were government ministers, media, cricket lovers, musicians and supporters and most of our family and friends. Vanessa had to work but her father, Rob, came up from Ballygarrett, County Wexford so that the kids could come out. Even Aunty Janet got the bus out from Foxrock to see us home. It truly was an amazing event.

The week was capped off by an appearance on 'The Late, Late Show' – they say if you make it onto this long-running RTÉ show you have made it. But the main event was the reception in the Shelbourne Hotel, put on by our major sponsor: Bank of Ireland. The evening was attended by An Taoiseach Bertie Ahern, who went away with an Irish cricket jersey to wear when he's next down in Croke Park. It was a fantastic event and reflected the support that the bank had given the players and the ICU. Tom Hayes made a lovely presentation to Adi, who spoke movingly about his time in charge. With typical selflessness, Adi invited Phil Simmons up onto the stage and passed the baton on to our new coach. It was a powerful moment, and yet another memory to store away with the most incredible four months of our lives. It was a time when fifteen men came together with one aim. With skill, determination, planning and hard work we showed the world, and the people back home, that Ireland could play cricket – and play it well!

SCORES AND STATISTICS

Group D
Ireland v Zimbabwe

Played at Sabina Park, Kingston, Jamaica, on 15 March 2007

Match tied

IRELAND		R	M	B	4s	6s
W Porterfield	Sibanda b Mpofu	0	4	6	0	0
J Bray	not out	115	221	137	10	2
E Morgan	c Chigumbura b Brent	21	37	27	4	0
+ N O'Brien	c Taylor b Chigumbura	1	3	5	0	0
A Botha	b Chigumbura	1	15	7	0	0
K O'Brien	c Taylor b Rainsford	10	33	28	2	0
A White	lbw b Brent	28	49	48	3	0
*T Johnston	run out (Williams/Mpofu)	20	49	24	2	0
K McCallan	st Taylor b Williams	0	2	3	0	0
D Langford-Smith	c Taylor b Mpofu	15	21	17	1	0
Extras	(b 1, lb 1, w 5, nb 3)	0				
Total	(9 wickets; 50 overs; 221 mins)	221				

Did not bat B Rankin

Fall: 1-0 (Porterfield, 0.6), 2-43 (Morgan, 9.5), 3-44 (N O'Brien, 10.4), 4-64 (Botha, 14.3), 5-89 (K O'Brien, 21.6), 6-145 (White, 37.3), 7-182 (Johnston, 43.6), 8-182 (McCallan, 44.3), 9-221 (Langford-Smith, 49.6)

	O	M	R	W	Econ
C Mpofu	10	3	58	2	5.80 (2w)
E Rainsford	7	0	44	1	6.28 (1nb, 1w)
E Chigumbura	6	2	21	2	3.50 (2nb)
G Brent	10	1	40	2	4.00 (2w)
P Utseya	10	0	29	0	2.90
S Williams	6	1	21	1	3.50
S Matsikenyeri	1	0	6	0	6.00

ZIMBABWE (target: 222 runs from 50 overs)		R	M	B	4s	6s
T Duffin	c N O'Brien b Rankin	12	23	22	2	0
V Sibanda	hit wicket b White	67	121	84	9	0
C Chibhabha	c Langford-Smith b Johnston	12	66	36	1	0
S Williams	c Rankin b McCallan	14	10	13	2	0
S Matsikenyeri	not out	73	122	76	9	1
E Chigumbura	c Bray b McCallan	4	5	9	0	0
+ B Taylor	run out (McCallan)	24	57	40	3	0
G Brent	lbw b Botha	3	15	12	0	0
* P Utseya	c Morgan b K O'Brien	1	3	3	0	0
C Mpofu	run out (Johnston/N O'Brien)	0	3	5	0	0
E Rainsford	run out (N O'Brien/White)	1	10	1	0	0
Extras	(lb 1, w 7, nb 2)	10				
Total	(all out; 50 overs)	221				

Fall: 1-26 (Duffin, 5.6), 2-92 (Chibhabha, 20.5), 3-107 (Williams, 23.2), 4-128 (Sibanda, 28.1), 5-133 (Chigumbura, 29.6), 6-203 (Taylor, 43.4), 7-212 (Brent, 47.3), 8-213 (Utseya, 48.1), 9-213 (Mpofu, 48.6), 10-221 (Rainsford, 49.6)

	O	M	R	W	Econ
D Langford-Smith	9	0	34	0	3.77 (5w)
B Rankin	7	1	43	1	6.14 (2w)
A Botha	10	2	32	1	3.20 (2nb)
T Johnston	10	2	32	1	3.20
K McCallan	9	1	56	2	6.22
A White	3	1	15	1	5.00
K O'Brien	2	1	8	1	4.00

Toss:	Zimbabwe, who chose to field first	
Umpires:	I Gould (England) and B Jerling (South Africa)	
Player of the match:	J Bray (Ireland)	Official Attendance: 2,011

» Jeremy Bray's 50 came off 64 balls (5x4, 2x6); 100 off 129 balls (10x4, 2x6)

Group D
Ireland v Pakistan

Played at Sabina Park, Kingston, Jamaica, on 17 March 2007
Ireland won by 3 wickets (with 32 balls remaining) (D/L method)

PAKISTAN		R	M	B	4s	6s
Imran Nazir	c Morgan b Botha	24	88	51	3	0
Mohammad Hafeez	c N O'Brien b Langford-Smith	4	5	6	I	0
Younis Khan	c Botha b Rankin	0	13	3	0	0
Mohammad Yousuf	c Porterfield b Johnston	15	43	31	2	0
* Inzamam-ul-Haq	c Morgan b Botha	I	2	3	0	0
Shoaib Malik	c N O'Brien b K O'Brien	9	32	25	2	0
+ Kamran Akmal	c Johnston b Rankin	27	56	47	4	0
Azhar Mahmood	c Johnston b Rankin	2	36	21	0	0
Mohammad Sami	c Bray b McCallan	12	51	34	I	0
Iftikhar Anjum	not out	8	55	43	0	0
Umar Gul	c sub (J Mooney) b McCallan	I	8	13	0	0
Extras	(lb 3, w 23, nb 3)	29				
Total	**(all out; 45.4 overs)**	**132**				

Fall: 1-7 (Hafeez, 0.6), 2-15 (Younis, 3.3), 3-56 (Yousuf, 12.5), 4-58 (Inzamam, 13.1), 5-66 (Imran, 17.6), 6-72 (Shoaib, 20.3), 7-103 (Azhar, 30.2), 8-105 (Kamran, 30.5), 9-130 (Sami, 43.1), 10-132 (Umar Gul, 45.4)

	O	M	R	W	Econ	
D Langford-Smith	10	I	31	I	3.10	(1nb, 5w)
B Rankin	9	I	32	3	3.55	(1nb, 13w)
A Botha	8	4	5	2	0.62	
T Johnston	7	I	20	I	2.85	(1nb, 4w)
K O'Brien	6	0	29	I	4.83	(1w)
K McCallan	5.4	I	12	2	2.11	

IRELAND (target: 128 runs from 47 overs)		R	M	B	4s	6s
J Bray	lbw b Mohammad Sami	3	14	13	0	0
W Porterfield	b Hafeez	13	100	50	I	0
E Morgan	lbw b Mohammad Sami	2	11	5	0	0
+ N O'Brien	st Kamran Akmal b Shoaib Malik	72	139	107	6	I
A Botha	c Hafeez b Sami	0	14	6	0	0
K O'Brien	not out	16	92	52	2	0
A White	c Hafeez b Iftikhar	4	3	3	I	0
K McCallan	c Younis Khan b Iftikhar Anjum	0	I	I	0	0
*T Johnston	not out	9	34	14	0	I
Extras	(lb 2, w 11, nb 1)	14				
Total	**(7 wickets; 41.4 overs)**	**133**				

Did not bat D Langford-Smith, B Rankin

Fall: 1-7 (Bray, 3.1), 2-15 (Morgan, 5.3), 3-62 (Porterfield, 20.6), 4-70 (Botha, 23.6), 5-108 (NJ O'Brien, 33.6), 6-113 (White, 34.5), 7-113 (McCallan, 34.6)

	O	M	R	W	Econ	
Umar Gul	9	0	24	0	2.66	(3w)
Mohammad Sami	10	0	29	3	2.90	(3w)
Iftikhar Anjum	10	0	29	2	2.90	(3w)
Azhar Mahmood	7.4	I	25	0	3.26	(2w)
Mohammad Hafeez	4	0	15	I	3.75	
Shoaib Malik	I	0	9	I	9.00	(1nb)

Toss:	Ireland, who chose to field first
Umpires:	B Bowden (New Zealand) and B Jerling (South Africa)
Player of the match:	N O'Brien (Ireland)

» Niall O'Brien's 50 came off 74 balls (4x4)

Official Attendance: 3,855

Group D
Ireland v West Indies

Played at Sabina Park, Kingston, Jamaica on 23 March 2007
West Indies won by 8 wickets (with 59 balls remaining) (D/L method)

IRELAND		R	M	B	4s	6s
J Bray	c sub (Simmons) b Taylor	41	105	72	7	0
W Porterfield	c Gayle b Powell	0	7	2	0	0
E Morgan	c Ramdin b Powell	18	66	34	0	1
+N O'Brien	c Ramdin b Bradshaw	11	21	19	2	0
A Botha	c Ramdin b Gayle	28	76	56	1	1
K O'Brien	c Sarwan b Gayle	17	51	46	1	0
A White	b Bravo	18	33	29	0	0
* K McCallan	not out	20	29	24	2	0
J Mooney	c Ramdin b Bravo	0	1	1	0	0
D Langford-Smith	not out	8	8	7	1	0
Extras	(b 4, lb 10, w 6, nb 2)	22				
Total	(8 wickets; 48 overs)	183				

Did not bat: B Rankin
Fall of wickets: 1-3 (Porterfield, 1.2), 2-61 (Morgan, 15.3), 3-76 (N O'Brien, 20.2), 4-82 (Bray, 21.6), 5-129 (K O'Brien, 35.4), 6-139 (Botha, 39.2), 7-163 (White, 45.5), 8-163 (Mooney, 45.6)

	O	M	R	W	Econ
J Taylor	8	0	37	1	4.62 (3w)
D Powell	9	2	24	2	2.66 (1w)
I Bradshaw	9	0	27	1	3.00
D Bravo	7	1	35	2	5.00 (2nb, 1w)
C Gayle	10	0	23	2	2.30 (1w)
M Samuels	5	0	23	0	4.60

WEST INDIES (target: 190 runs from 48 overs)		R	M	B	4s	6s
C Gayle	c White b Langford-Smith	18	20	14	3	0
S Chanderpaul	not out	102	161	113	10	4
R Sarwan	c K O'Brien b McCallan	36	97	71	2	1
M Samuels	not out	27	41	31	2	2
Extras	(lb 1, w 6)	7				
Total	(2 wkts; 38.1 overs; 161 mins)	190				

Did not bat: B Lara, D Bravo, D Smith, D Ramdin, I Bradshaw, J Taylor, D Powell
Fall of wickets: 1-24 (Gayle, 4.3), 2-143 (Sarwan, 27.4)

	O	M	R	W	Econ
D Langford-Smith	9	1	33	1	3.66 (3w)
B Rankin	5	0	38	0	7.60 (2w)
A Botha	6	0	35	0	5.83
J Mooney	4	1	22	0	5.50
K McCallan	10	0	35	1	3.50 (1w)
K O'Brien	3	0	13	0	4.33
A White	1.1	0	13	0	11.14

Toss: Ireland, who chose to bat first
Player of the match: S Chanderpaul (West Indies)
Umpires: B Bowden (New Zealand) and I Gould (England)

Official Attendance: 11,997

Super Eights
Ireland v England

Played at Providence Stadium, Guyana, on 30 March 2007
England won by 48 runs

ENGLAND		R	M	B	4s	6s
E Joyce	b Rankin	1	5	5	0	0
* M Vaughan	c N O'Brien b Rankin	6	27	13	1	0
IR Bell	c N O'Brien b K O'Brien	31	92	74	2	0
KP Pietersen	c Porterfield b McCallan	48	91	47	5	0
PD Collingwood	run out (White/Johnston)	90	118	82	8	3
A Flintoff	b Johnston	43	64	62	4	0
+ PA Nixon	c Morgan b Botha	19	23	15	1	1
RS Bopara	not out	10	9	5	1	0
SI Mahmood	not out	0	1	0	0	0
Extras	(lb 2, w 13, nb 3)	18				
Total	**(7 wickets; 50 overs)**	**266**				

Did not bat: JM Anderson, MS Panesar
Fall: 1-6 (Joyce, 1.1), 2-23 (Vaughan, 5.2), 3-89 (Bell, 21.2), 4-113 (Pietersen, 26.3), 5-194 (Flintoff, 43.3), 6-245 (Nixon, 48.2), 7-258 (Collingwood, 49.3)

	O	M	R	W	Econ
D Langford-Smith	7	0	38	0	5.42 (3nb, 3w)
B Rankin	7	1	28	2	4.00 (4w)
T Johnston	10	0	70	1	7.00
A Botha	10	1	56	1	5.60
K O'Brien	4	0	26	1	6.50 (2w)
K McCallan	10	0	38	1	3.80 (2w)
A White	2	0	8	0	4.00

IRELAND (target: 267 runs from 50 overs)		R	M	B	4s	6s
W Porterfield	c Bell b Flintoff	31	84	68	1	0
J Bray	c Bopara b Anderson	0	1	1	0	0
E Morgan	run out (Mahmood)	2	12	7	0	0
+N O'Brien	st Nixon b Vaughan	63	128	88	4	0
A Botha	c Flintoff b Panesar	18	34	39	1	0
K O'Brien	lbw b Panesar	12	19	19	1	0
*T Johnston	b Flintoff	27	34	21	1	2
A White	c Nixon b Collingwood	38	39	35	4	0
K McCallan	b Flintoff	5	16	6	0	0
D Langford-Smith	lbw b Flintoff	1	1	2	0	0
B Rankin	not out	4	8	8	0	0
Extras	(lb 3, w 9, nb 5)	17				
Total	**(all out; 48.1 overs)**	**218**				

Fall: 1-6 (Bray, 0.5), 2-11 (Morgan, 3.4), 3-72 (Porterfield, 18.5), 4-116 (Botha, 29.5), 5-139 (K O'Brien, 35.6), 6-139 (N O'Brien, 36.2), 7-197 (Johnston, 44.5), 8-209 (White, 45.5), 9-210 (Langford-Smith, 46.1), 10-218 (McCallan, 48.1)

	O	M	R	W	Econ
J Anderson	7	1	35	1	5.00 (4w)
S Mahmood	8	2	34	0	4.25 (1nb, 1w)
A Flintoff	8.1	1	43	4	5.26 (4nb)
P Collingwood	6	0	38	1	6.33 (1w)
M Panesar	10	1	31	2	3.10
M Vaughan	9	0	34	1	3.77 (1w)

Toss: England, who chose to bat first
Umpires: B Doctrove and S Taufel (Australia)
Player of the match: P Collingwood (England)   Official Attendance: 4,800
» Niall O'Brien's 50 came off 66 balls (4x4)

Super Eights
Ireland v South Africa
Played at Providence Stadium, Guyana, on 3 April 2007
South Africa won by 7 wickets (with 21 balls remaining) (D/L method)

IRELAND

		R	M	B	4s	6s
JP Bray	lbw b Pollock	0	10	9	0	0
W Porterfield	c Kallis b Pollock	14	44	33	1	0
E Morgan	c Prince b Hall	28	64	50	4	0
+N O'Brien	c Gibbs b Langeveldt	25	44	37	3	0
A White	c Gibbs b Smith	30	30	30	5	0
A Botha	c de Villiers b Hall	14	31	20	0	0
* T Johnston	not out	13	37	14	0	1
K McCallan	c Boucher b Langeveldt	3	5	6	0	0
P Mooney	c Boucher b Langeveldt	0	1	1	0	0
D Langford-Smith	not out	17	14	10	1	1
Extras	(b 1, lb 3, w 4)	8				
Total	**(8 wickets; 35 overs)**	**152**				

Did not bat: B Rankin
Fall: 1-0 (Bray, 2.3), 2-31 (Porterfield, 12.3), 3-63 (Morgan, 19.5), 4-77 (O'Brien, 22.5), 5-116 (White, 28.6), 6-119 (Botha, 30.1), 7-124 (McCallan, 31.3), 8-124 (Mooney, 31.4)

	O	M	R	W	Econ	
S Pollock	7	2	17	2	2.42	
M Ntini	7	2	14	0	2.00	(2w)
C Langeveldt	7	0	41	3	5.85	(2w)
A Hall	7	0	37	2	5.28	
J Kemp	3	0	14	0	4.66	
J Kallis	3	0	20	0	6.66	
G Smith	1	0	5	1	5.00	

SOUTH AFRICA (target: 160 runs from 35 overs)

		R	M	B	4s	6s
A de Villiers	c Porterfield b Rankin	0	1	3	0	0
G Smith	c & b Johnston	41	56	45	6	0
J Kallis	not out	66	138	86	8	0
H Gibbs	c White b Rankin	6	19	15	1	0
A Prince	not out	47	61	44	3	1
Extras	(w 1, nb 4)	5				
Total	**(3 wickets; 31.3 overs)**	**165**				

Did not bat: MV Boucher, JM Kemp, SM Pollock, AJ Hall, CK Langeveldt, M Ntini
Fall: 1-1 (de Villiers, 0.3), 2-71 (Smith, 12.1), 3-85 (Gibbs, 16.3)

	O	M	R	W	Econ	
B Rankin	7	1	26	2	3.71	(1nb, 1w)
D Langford-Smith	5	0	31	0	6.20	
P Mooney	3.3	0	40	0	11.42	(3nb)
T Johnston	3	0	15	1	5.00	
A Botha	6	0	18	0	3.00	
K McCallan	5	0	27	0	5.40	
A White	2	0	8	0	4.00	

Toss:	South Africa, who chose to field first
Umpires:	D Harper (Australia) and S Taufel (Australia)
Player of the match:	JH Kallis (South Africa)

Official Attendance: 5,673

Super Eights

Ireland v New Zealand

Played at Providence Stadium, Guyana, on 9 April 2007
New Zealand won by 129 runs

NEW ZEALAND		R	M	B	4s	6s
P Fulton	lbw b McCallan	83	160	110	9	0
*S Fleming	c Porterfield b Rankin	10	26	11	1	0
H Marshall	c Morgan b Langford-Smith	16	21	21	2	0
S Styris	c N O'Brien b Langford-Smith	10	25	15	1	0
C McMillan	c Johnston b McCallan	22	29	29	1	1
J Oram	c Morgan b White	20	78	48	0	0
+B McCullum	c Morgan b Johnston	47	49	37	2	1
D Vettori	c N O'Brien b White	5	6	7	0	0
J Franklin	not out	34	31	22	3	1
S Bond	not out	0	1	0	0	0
Extras	(b 3, lb 1, w 12)	16				
Total	**(8 wickets; 50 overs)**	**263**				

Did not bat: J Patel

Fall: 1-35 (Fleming, 5.4), 2-59 (Marshall, 10.6), 3-83 (Styris, 16.3), 4-118 (McMillan, 24.4), 5-172 (Fulton, 38.1), 6-181 (Oram, 40.4), 7-189 (Vettori, 42.3), 8-260 (McCullum, 49.4)

	O	M	R	W	Econ	
D Langford-Smith	10	1	41	2	4.10 (1w)	
B Rankin	8	0	55	1	6.87 (7w)	
T Johnston	10	0	63	1	6.30 (1w)	
K McCallan	10	0	35	2	3.50 (1w)	
A White	10	0	45	2	4.50	
K O'Brien	2	0	20	0	10.00	

IRELAND (target: 264 runs from 50 overs)		R	M	B	4s	6s
W Porterfield	c Styris b Bond	11	32	22	0	0
J Bray	c McCullum b Bond	1	7	5	0	0
E Morgan	c McCullum b Oram	15	46	37	2	0
+N O'Brien	c Oram b Patel	30	109	75	2	0
K J O'Brien	run out (Styris/Marshall)	49	67	45	2	3
*T Johnston	lbw b Patel	13	27	19	1	0
A White	lbw b Vettori	0	2	4	0	0
P Gillespie	lbw b Vettori	2	8	8	0	0
K McCallan	b Vettori	0	9	8	0	0
D Langford-Smith	not out	0	6	4	0	0
B Rankin	lbw b Vettori	0	2	1	0	0
Extras	(lb 3, w 8, nb 2)	13				
Total	**(all out; 37.4 overs)**	**134**				

Fall: 1-5 (Bray, 1.6), 2-22 (Porterfield, 7.2), 3-35 (Morgan, 12.5), 4-110 (K O'Brien, 28.4), 5-125 (N O'Brien, 32.3), 6-127 (White, 33.3), 7-133 (Johnston, 34.4), 8-133 (Gillespie, 35.5), 9-134 (McCallan, 37.3), 10-134 (Rankin, 37.4)

	O	M	R	W	Econ	
JEC Franklin	8	1	27	0	3.37 (1nb)	
SE Bond	5	0	18	2	3.60 (1nb, 2w)	
JDP Oram	6	2	15	1	2.50 (1w)	
JS Patel	7	1	32	2	4.57	
DL Vettori	8.4	1	23	4	2.65 (1w)	
SB Styris	3	0	16	0	5.33	

Toss: New Zealand, who chose to bat first
Umpires: S Bucknor (WI) and S Taufel (Australia)
Player of the match: P Fulton (New Zealand)   Official Attendance: 6,500

Super Eights
Ireland v Australia

Played at Kensington Oval, Bridgetown, Barbados, on 13 April 2007
Australia won by 9 wickets (with 226 balls remaining)

IRELAND		R	M	B	4s	6s
J Bray	b McGrath	1	3	2	0	0
W Porterfield	lbw b Tait	1	14	11	0	0
E Morgan	c Hayden b McGrath	0	19	9	0	0
+N O'Brien	b Tait	0	1	1	0	0
K O'Brien	c Hodge b Clark	16	51	25	3	0
A White	c Hogg b McGrath	6	30	20	0	0
*T Johnston	b Tait	17	30	25	2	0
K McCallan	c Tait b Symonds	5	32	18	0	0
J Mooney	run out (Tait)	23	53	44	2	0
D Langford-Smith	c Ponting b Hogg	2	8	7	0	0
B Rankin	not out	4	25	19	0	0
Extras	(w 15, nb 1)	16				
Total	**(all out; 30 overs; 138 mins)**	**91**				

Fall: 1-2 (Bray, 0.6), 2-2 (Porterfield, 3.1), 3-2 (N O'Brien, 3.2), 4-12 (Morgan, 4.3), 5-32 (White, 10.3), 6-42 (K O'Brien, 13.2), 7-54 (Johnston, 16.3), 8-72 (McCallan, 20.6), 9-80 (Langford-Smith, 23.1), 10-91 (Mooney, 29.6)

	O	M	R	W	Econ	
G McGrath	7	1	17	3	2.42	
S Tait	6	1	39	3	6.50 (1nb, 9w)	
S Clark	8	1	19	1	2.37 (1w)	
B Hogg	6	2	9	1	1.50 (2w)	
A Symonds	3	1	7	1	2.33	

AUSTRALIA (target: 92 runs from 50 overs)		R	M	B	4s	6s
+A Gilchrist	b Johnston	34	38	25	4	0
M Hussey	not out	30	57	41	3	1
A Symonds	not out	15	17	9	1	1
Extras	(lb 4, w 8, nb 1)	13				
Total	**(1 wicket; 12.2 overs; 57 mins)**	**92**				

Did not bat: M Hayden, *R Ponting, M Clarke, B Hodge, B Hogg, S Clark, S Tait, G McGrath
Fall: 1-62 (Gilchrist, 8.5)

	O	M	R	W	Econ	
D Langford-Smith	3	0	27	0	9.00 (2w)	
B Rankin	4.2	0	24	0	5.53 (4w)	
T Johnston	3	0	18	1	6.00 (1nb, 2w)	
J Mooney	1	0	14	0	14.00	
K McCallan	1	0	5	0	5.00	

Toss:	Australia, who chose to field first
Umpires:	B Bowden (New Zealand) and R Koertzen (South Africa)
Player of the match:	GD McGrath (Australia)

Official Attendance: 12,178

183

Super Eights

Ireland v Bangladesh

Played at Kensington Oval, Bridgetown, Barbados, on 15 April 2007
Ireland won by 74 runs

IRELAND		R	M	B	4s	6s
W Porterfield	c Rafique b Mortaza	85	175	136	3	0
J Bray	run out (Saqibul/Mushfiqur)	31	111	70	1	0
E Morgan	run out (Mushfiqur/Shahadat)	5	7	9	1	0
+N O'Brien	c Tamim Iqbal b Saqibul Hasan	10	21	14	0	0
K O'Brien	run out (sub [Farhad]/Mushfiqur)	48	58	44	2	2
*T Johnston	c Shahriar b Mortaza	30	38	23	2	1
A White	run out (sub [Farhad]/Mushfiqur)	4	6	4	0	0
D Langford-Smith	not out	6	7	4	1	0
A Botha	not out	1	2	1	0	0
Extras	(b 1, lb 11, w 6, nb 5)	23				
Total	**(7 wickets; 50 overs; 220 mins)**	**243**				

Did not bat: K McCallan, B Rankin
Fall: 1-92 (Bray, 25.3), 2-101 (Morgan, 27.5), 3-128 (N O'Brien, 33.2), 4-176 (Porterfield, 41.3), 5-215 (K O'Brien, 47.1), 6-233 (White, 48.5), 7-237 (Johnston, 49.3)

	O	M	R	W	Econ
Mashrafe Mortaza	10	1	38	2	3.80 (3nb)
Shahadat Hossain	9	1	51	0	5.66 (2nb, 1w)
Abdur Razzak	9	0	48	0	5.33 (2w)
Mohammad Rafique	10	0	42	0	4.20 (2w)
Saqibul Hasan	10	0	44	1	4.40
Aftab Ahmed	2	0	8	0	4.00 (1w)

BANGLADESH (target: 244 runs from 50 overs)		R	M	B	4s	6s
Tamim Iqbal	b Johnston	29	96	59	4	0
Shahriar Nafees	c N O'Brien b Rankin	7	29	18	1	0
Aftab Ahmed	c N O'Brien b Botha	12	20	9	1	1
Saqibul Hasan	run out (Botha)	3	12	8	0	0
Mohammad Ashraful	c Langford-Smith b Rankin	35	43	36	5	1
*Habibul Bashar	b Johnston	32	92	57	2	0
+Mushfiqur Rahim	b McCallan	16	31	26	2	0
Mashrafe Mortaza	c & b Langford-Smith	0	5	3	0	0
Mohammad Rafique	c Johnston b Langford-Smith	2	9	9	0	0
Abdur Razzak	b McCallan	11	29	21	0	0
Shahadat Hossain	not out	0	3	2	0	0
Extras	(lb 4, w 18)	22				
Total	**(all out; 41.2 overs; 189 mins)**	**169**				

Fall: 1-18 (Shahriar Nafees, 6.3), 2-45 (Aftab Ahmed, 10.1), 3-48 (Saqibul Hasan, 12.4), 4-93 (Tamim Iqbal, 19.6), 5-102 (Mohammad Ashraful, 21.6), 6-131 (Mushfiqur Rahim, 30.4), 7-134 (Mashrafe Mortaza, 31.2), 8-138 (Mohammad Rafique, 33.4), 9-169 (Abdur Razzak, 40.4), 10-169 (Habibul Bashar, 41.2)

	O	M	R	W	Econ
B Rankin	8	0	42	2	5.25 (9w)
D Langford-Smith	10	1	27	2	2.70 (3w)
A Botha	8	0	31	1	3.87
T Johnston	7.2	0	40	2	5.45 (2w)
K McCallan	8	1	25	2	3.12

Toss: Ireland, who chose to bat first
Umpires: B Bowden (New Zealand) and S Bucknor (West Indies)
Player of the match: W Porterfield (Ireland)   Official Attendance: 15,541
» William Porterfield's 50 came off 88 balls (3x4)

Super Eights
Ireland v Sri Lanka
Played at National Cricket Stadium, St George's, Grenada, on 18 April 2007
Sri Lanka won by 8 wickets (with 240 balls remaining)

IRELAND		R	M	B	4s	6s
J Bray	c Arnold b Maharoof	20	32	29	4	0
W Porterfield	c Jayasuriya b Maharoof	17	79	51	1	0
A Botha	c Sangakkara b Maharoof	0	2	2	0	0
E Morgan	c Sangakkara b Maharoof	0	1	1	0	0
+N O'Brien	c Sangakkara b Muralitharan	4	46	28	0	0
K O'Brien	c Jayasuriya b Muralitharan	2	14	4	0	0
K Carroll	b Muralitharan	0	1	2	0	0
*T Johnston	run out (Maharoof)	0	5	4	0	0
K McCallan	lbw b Muralitharan	0	10	9	0	0
D Langford-Smith	lbw b Vaas	18	29	21	2	1
B Rankin	not out	7	20	17	1	0
Extras	(lb 5, w 2, nb 2)	9				
Total	(all out; 27.4 overs; 125 mins)	77				

Fall: 1-28 (Bray, 7.3), 2-28 (Botha, 7.5), 3-28 (Morgan, 7.6), 4-46 (Porterfield, 17.6), 5-48 (N O'Brien, 18.2), 6-48 (Carroll, 18.4), 7-49 (Johnston, 19.4), 8-49 (K O'Brien, 20.1), 9-54 (McCallan, 22.4), 10-77 (Langford-Smith, 27.4)

	O	M	R	W	Econ
C Vaas	5.4	1	18	1	3.17 (1nb)
N Kulasekara	7	3	10	0	1.42
M Maharoof	10	3	25	4	2.50 (1nb)
M Muralitharan	5	0	19	4	3.80 (2w)

SRI LANKA (target: 78 runs from 50 overs)		R	M	B	4s	6s
U Tharanga	c Porterfield b Rankin	0	5	7	0	0
S Jayasuriya	not out	24	51	20	3	1
+K Sangakkara	c Carroll b Langford-Smith	10	15	9	1	0
* M Jayawardene	not out	39	30	27	6	1
Extras	(w 5, nb 3)	8				
Total	(2 wickets; 10 overs; 51 mins)	81				

Did not bat: L Silva, T Dilshan, R Arnold, M Maharoof, C Vaas, K Kulasekara, M Muralitharan
Fall: 1-1 (Tharanga, 0.6), 2-25 (Sangakkara, 3.2)

	O	M	R	W	Econ
B Rankin	4	0	36	1	9.00 (3nb, 2w)
D Langford-Smith	3	0	29	1	9.66 (3w)
A Botha	1	0	4	0	4.00
K O'Brien	1	0	4	0	4.00
K Carroll	1	0	8	0	8.00

Toss:	Sri Lanka, who chose to field first
Umpires:	M Benson (England) and B Doctrove (West Indies)
Player of the match:	M Maharoof (Sri Lanka)

Official Attendance: 7,335

Batting averages

	Mts	Inns	NO	Runs	HS	Ave	BF	SR	100	50	0s	4s	6s
J Bray	9	9	1	212	115*	26.50	338	62.72	1	0	2	22	2
K O'Brien	8	8	1	170	49	24.28	263	64.63	0	0	0	13	5
N O'Brien	9	9	0	216	72	24.00	374	57.75	0	2	1	17	1
T Johnston	8	8	2	129	30	21.50	144	89.58	0	0	1	8	5
W Porterfield	9	9	0	172	85	19.11	379	45.38	0	1	2	7	0
D Langford-Smith	9	8	4	67	18	16.75	72	93.05	0	0	0	6	2
A White	8	8	0	128	38	16.00	173	73.98	0	0	1	13	0
B Rankin	9	4	3	15	7*	15.00	45	33.33	0	0	1	1	0
J Mooney	2	2	0	23	23	11.50	45	51.11	0	0	1	2	0
A Botha	7	7	1	62	28	10.33	131	47.32	0	0	2	2	1
E Morgan	9	9	0	91	28	10.11	179	50.83	0	0	2	11	1
K McCallan	9	8	1	33	20*	4.71	75	44.00	0	0	4	2	0
P Gillespie	1	1	0	2	2	2.00	8	25.00	0	0	0	0	0
K Carroll	1	1	0	0	0	0.00	2	0.00	0	0	1	0	0
P Mooney	1	1	0	0	0	0.00	1	0.00	0	0	1	0	0

Mts= matches; Inns= innings; NO= not outs; HS= Highest score; Ave= average; BF= balls faced; SR= scoring rate (runs per 100 balls). The final five columns refer to the number of centuries, fifties and ducks scored by each batsman, and the number of boundary fours and sixes hit.

Bowling averages

	IB	Overs	Mdns	Runs	Wkts	BBI	Ave	Econ	SR
K McCallan	8	58.4	3	233	10	2/12	23.30	3.97	35.2
B Rankin	9	59.2	4	324	12	3/32	27.00	5.46	29.6
A White	5	18.1	1	89	3	2/45	29.66	4.89	36.3
T Johnston	7	50.2	3	258	8	2/40	32.25	5.12	37.7
K O'Brien	6	18.0	1	100	3	1/8	33.33	5.55	36.0
A Botha	7	49.0	7	181	5	2/5	36.20	3.69	58.8
D Langford-Smith	9	66.0	4	291	7	2/27	41.57	4.40	56.5
K Carroll	1	1.0	0	8	0	-	-	8.00	-
J Mooney	2	5.0	1	36	0	-	-	7.20	-
P Mooney	1	3.3	0	40	0	-	-	11.42	-

IB= innings bowled; Mdns= maiden overs; Wkts= wickets; BBI= best bowling in an innings; Ave = average; Econ= economy rate (runs per over); SR= strike rate (balls per wicket)

Catches: N O'Brien 9, E Morgan 7, T Johnston 5, W Porterfield 5, D Langford-Smith 3, A White 2, J Bray 2, K Carroll 1, A Botha 1, K O'Brien 1, B Rankin 1, substitute (J Mooney) 1

Group D
final table

	P	W	L	T	NR	Pts	Net RR
West Indies	3	3	0	0	0	6	+0.764
Ireland	**3**	**1**	**1**	**1**	**0**	**3**	**-0.092**
Pakistan	3	1	2	0	0	2	+0.089
Zimbabwe	3	0	2	1	0	1	-0.886

Super Eights
final table

	P	W	L	T	NR	Pts	Net RR
Australia	7	7	0	0	0	14	+2.400
Sri Lanka	7	5	2	0	0	10	+1.483
New Zealand	7	5	2	0	0	10	+0.253
South Africa	7	4	3	0	0	8	+0.313
England	7	3	4	0	0	6	-0.394
West Indies	7	2	5	0	0	4	-0.566
Bangladesh	7	1	6	0	0	2	-1.514
Ireland	**7**	**1**	**6**	**0**	**0**	**2**	**-1.730**

ICC One-day International
World Rankings

(12 May 2007)

		Matches	Points	Rating
1	Australia	54	7038	130
2	South Africa	43	5313	124
3	New Zealand	45	5103	113
4	Sri Lanka	53	5879	111
5	Pakistan	36	3950	110
6	India	52	5553	107
7	England	43	4457	104
8	West Indies	47	4666	99
9	Bangladesh	44	1962	45
10	**Ireland**	**11**	**317**	**29**
11	Zimbabwe	36	779	22
12	Kenya	11	0	0

Trent Johnston's Senior Career Record

All matches for Ireland (2004 to end of 2007 season)

M	Inn	NO	Runs	Avge	HS	Wkts	Runs	Average
63	59	10	1231	25.12	83	96	2283	23.77

7 fifties, 26 catches, 2 five-wicket innings, 6-23 best bowling

One-day Internationals for Ireland (2006-2007)

M	Inn	NO	Runs	Avge	HS	Wkts	Runs	Average
17	15	4	275	25.00	45*	10	552	55.20

9 catches, 2-40 best bowling

First Class matches for New South Wales (1998-2000)

M	Inn	NO	Runs	Avge	HS	Wkts	Runs	Average
5	9	3	44	6.50	21	6	412	68.66

1 catch, 2-50 best bowling

Sydney Grade Cricket for Campbelltown, North Sydney and Mosman (1995-2004)

M	Inn	NO	Runs	Avge	HS	Wkts	Runs	Average
158	137	19	2,516	21.32	115	348	7,119	20.45

6-25 best bowling

Leinster club cricket for Carlisle, Leinster, Clontarf and Railway Union (1995-2007)

M	Inn	NO	Runs	Avge	HS	Wkts	Runs	Average
117	108	19	3,950	44.38	140*	240	3,882	16.09

10 Centuries, 21 Fifties, 8 Five wicket innings, 74 Catches, 7-25 best bowling

Gerard Siggins's senior career record

Leinster club cricket for Dublin University (1988)

M	Inn	NO	Runs	Avge	HS	Wkts	Runs	Average
1	0	-	0	-	-	0	-	-

0 Catches

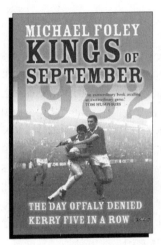

Kings of September

The Day Offaly Denied Kerry Five in a Row

Michael Foley

On the 19 September 1982 Mick O'Dwyer's Kerry ran out in Croke Park chasing immortality. Victory over Offaly in the All-Ireland football final would secure them five titles in a row, a record certain never to be matched again. And it had taken Offaly six heartbreaking years under manager Eugene McGee to drag themselves up from their lowest ebb, but now they stood on the cusp of a glorious reward. The result was a classic final that changed lives and dramatically altered the course of football history. *The Kings of September* is an epic story of triumph and loss, joy and tragedy, a story of two teams that illuminated a grim period in Irish life and enthralled a nation.

The Dirty Dozen

Ireland's Motorsport Legends

John Kenny

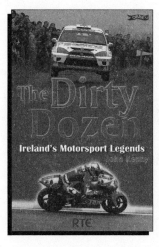

What drives them? Twelve of Ireland's legendary motor-sports stars speak about the highs and lows of their sport, whether scorching up the stages in rallying, the perilous thrills of motorbikes or the glamour and high stakes of circuit racing. Ruthless determination to get in front while at the same time blocking the driver or rider behind causes bitter rivalries, shocking injuries and sometimes even sabotage, but bravery, teamwork and sheer exhiliaration also have their part to play.

Rally: Billy Coleman, Paddy Hopkirk, Austin MacHale and Rosemary Smith.

Bikes: The Dunlop Brothers and Jeremy McWilliams.

Circuit: Derek Daly, Martin Donnelly, Eddie Irvine, Eddie Jordan, Michael Roe, John Watson.